NEUROSIS AND CRIME

FRANCES SMART

NEUROSIS & CRIME

edited by B. CURTIS BROWN

BARNES & NOBLE, INC.

NEW YORK, NEW YORK

First published in the United States, 1970
by Barnes & Noble, Inc.

SBN 389 01360 9

Printed in Great Britain

CONTENTS

CONTENTS

The views expressed in this book are the writer's
and do not necessarily represent those of the
Home Office.

FOREWORD

THIS BOOK, the outcome of ten years' practical experience by the late Dr. Frances Smart as a Visiting Psychotherapist at Wormwood Scrubs, is, I believe, the first book to have been written in this country about psychotherapy in prisons. Dr. Smart was a very dedicated prison psychotherapist, and her book is a valuable contribution to the growing accumulation of psychiatric knowledge about the treatment of criminal offenders.

The psychiatric treatment of prisoners is still very new and in the Prison Service of England and Wales dates only from the 1930s: in particular from the publication of the Report on the Psychological Treatment of Crime by the late Sir Norwood East and Dr. W. H. de B. Hubert published in 1939. Suitable patients are selected by prison medical officers and can be referred to the specialists at Wormwood Scrubs from any prison establishment. There is, however, an increasing interest in forensic psychiatry and there are now psychotherapists working in many other centres besides Wormwood Scrubs.

While psychotherapy can be of benefit only to a limited number of prisoners, even by using group and community therapy methods, these are often the most troubled, and troublesome, inmates. Dr. Smart rightly stresses that the psychiatrist is concerned with the individual patient.

I. G. W. Pickering, V.R.D., M.D., M.R.C.P.,
Director of Prison Medical Services, Home Office.

vii

"I have the highest opinion of her capacity to understand the human soul."

Prof. C. A. Meier
Formerly President and Director of the
G. C. Jung Institute, Zürich

PREFACE

Frances Emma Smart was born on May 13th 1909 and graduated as M.B., Ch.B. from Birmingham University in 1932. She consolidated her training by a three-year period of house jobs held successively at the Birmingham Children's, Maternity and General Hospitals and then worked for ten years in general practice. She had become increasingly interested in the study of mental illness and in 1945 decided to make this her chief work; so she moved to London to study for Part 1 of the Diploma of Psychological Medicine, which she gained in 1947. Then followed three years of study in Zürich under C. G. Jung and Professor C. A. Meier (who subsequently became President of the C. G. Jung Institute), and in 1951 she gained the Analyst's Diploma of the C. G. Jung Institute—being, in fact, the first to achieve this distinction. When she returned to England she completed her study for the D.P.M. and thereafter held appointments at Bowden House, the Metropolitan Hospital and the Paddington Clinic and Day Hospital, as well as treating private patients. She also lectured to students training with the Society of Analytical Psychology. A turning-point in her work was her appointment, in 1957, as visiting psycho-therapist to H.M. Prison, Wormwood Scrubs. This work became her dominant interest and in order to devote herself to it more intensively she gradually gave up the greater part of her private practice.

When Dr. Smart died on April 10th 1968, she had just begun the writing of the final section of this book—the section which was to deal with her treatment by individual psychotherapy of prisoner-patients, its results, her conclusions and, finally, the philosophy which underlay her methods. This section was, of course, to be the culmination of the book and as it became clear during the last few months of her life that her illness was to prove fatal and that there might scarcely be time to complete the book she omitted, or left unfinished, some chapters which immediately preceded this last section, hoping that it might be possible to return to them later. Also, she asked me to draft an Introduction from notes she gave me and which she expected to add to later. Tragically, the end came even more rapidly than we expected and, as will be seen, the incomplete chapters remained unfinished and one chapter (to deal with cases where treatment had failed and the reasons for this) was never even mapped out. Neither did she live to read the Introduction I had drafted. This, therefore, now consists of her notes which I have simply expanded from the bare note form, for intelligibility or flow, supplemented by a very few passages which she had written but not yet incorporated into the book, and which seemed to me to extend her notes in the way she was planning to do. The present Introduction is therefore authentic—her own statement about the book.

She left chapter headings for two of the final chapters as well as subheadings for the chapters on Treatment (Chapters 11 and 12). A note on my method of completing and editing these and Chapter 13, will be found in Chapter 11 where her own writing breaks off. The gaps—passages for which there was no written material to draw on—will be obvious and are grievous; but I am hopeful that there are no essential links missing in the line of thought or in communication. What has been difficult to avoid, however, is some appearance of repetition here and there—at least in emphasis. There is, for instance, the recurring reference to the importance of the mother-infant relation. This is more conspicuous at the end of the book, where I have had to rely on her notes alone and did not feel justified in paring down or proportioning anything previously written by her before her death in order to bring the additional material into balance. Nevertheless, this factor—which she believed gave the pattern to each individual's development—had for her the very greatest importance as a cause of neurosis and in the treatment of antisocial or criminal behaviour. One of her notes runs, "The majority of my patients have a history of rejection or otherwise unsatisfactory relationship with the mother." And a sentence near the end of Chapter 15, *What Lies Behind Treatment*, puts her view even more strongly, "Emotional stability and maturity in a young mother ... is a goal at least as important for the mental health of future generations as social reform."

But in accounting for the cases of possible repetition, as for other instances of constructional or stylistic imperfection, I can only say that as death came so soon she was not able to give a final revision to the typescript, though each chapter was re-read and revised as the book's writing proceeded. And no editor, I believe, would have taken it upon himself to disturb, even by minor changes, what had been set down with such thought and deliberation, when the writer was no longer there to sanction changes.

There is one other point which may need explanation—and which I believe Dr. Smart herself would have commented on had she completed her Introduction. That is, that although an important part of the book deals with the development of the normal personality and with factors which can disturb this— all of which is equally applicable to men or women, to the law-abiding or the law-breaker—this is primarily a book about work in a *men's* prison. It is from the men and boys she treated in prison that she draws her examples and it is their problems which here provide material for her analysis of cause and effect and her conclusions on the relation of neurosis to crime. I feel it may be necessary to emphasize this since some readers may be led to seek information, on some specific point, which is not here. I myself, for instance, when working on the book with her, said at one point, "What you are saying about individual development and the disturbed personality is equally true of women. Yet the social effects might be quite different in the case of women. You haven't made a single reference to women." She replied that she did intend to quote some examples from cases of women patients at the end of the book (I suspect this would have come in the chapter on the philosophy behind method) but that these would have to be taken from her work outside prison.

It will be clear, of course, that the total intention of the book reaches beyond the study of prison cases; nevertheless, it is this particular experience—prison work—which prompted the book and gives it its framework: this was the book she wished at this time to write. I believe others may feel, as I do myself, that by limiting this book to her work with prisoners, the universality of her theme is—paradoxically—made more manifest. But this limiting does mean, of course, that there are many questions for which she was not intending, here, to provide answers. As she wrote in the notes for her introduction, "I do not set out to establish a standard and I have made no attempt to be definitive or encyclopaedic."

But in spite of the obvious gaps and omissions, in spite even of the fact that the writing of the book was broken off by death at the most crucial point so that the last section is knit together from her notebooks and other writings, I believe that what is here will still bear witness to the fertilizing and devoted work of this doctor, the basis of whose treatment was love and humility and whose aim was the release of the disabled personality to accept the responsibilities of living. I believe also that it will go far to carry out her intention, which was to share her knowledge of the human spirit with others and to open our understanding towards those whose nurture had distorted their personality, who are fettered in their immaturity and who, unlike those of us who remain within the law, have had no counterbalancing element in their lives to strengthen them in handling neuroses and instincts—from which, after all, few if any of us can claim to be immune.

I have, I hope, succeeded in not stepping from the professional into the personal area where this was not germane to the substance of the book. But I found I had also to consider that a living writer can be, as it were, called to account: his (or her) integrity as a witness can be tested by actual contact with his personality, if necessary. The validity of a book of this kind, in particular, is underwritten by the character of the writer. For this reason I have felt it was impossible not to include at least an impression of Frances Smart as a personality and to try to convey something of the impression she made on others. But I do not feel that this Introduction is the right place for it and it would be improper to divert the subject and purpose of such a book as this towards the personality of the writer. (Where personal comments upon her or her work are included in the body of the book, it is because these throw light on her methods.) But since I felt that a personal picture could not be omitted I have put this in an Appendix at the end of the book.

I should perhaps explain my own part in this book. Dr. Smart felt diffident about her capacity for communicating to the lay reader in *writing*. Her profession, as well as her nature, made her a listener above all and she was a most skilled oral communicator. But when it came to writing, she said, she dreaded even letters. As I am a writer and journalist and have had a good deal of experience in helping others to write on various subjects, and as we were old friends and could understand each other's intentions in speech or writing, I offered to help her in planning the structure of the book and in easing the expression where this was needed for the lay reader. We worked very closely together and at her death I was asked to complete the book so far as I could from what materials she left. As I have said, I have set out as fully as I could how I have done the work, in Chapter 12. The only chapter which was not originally intended for the book is the final one, which is a lecture she gave some years ago. I felt that this should be included because, in the first place, it filled some of the gaps which had been left in the material available to me and, in the second place, because being a piece intended for speech, it makes a more informal, direct and personal impact and so brings the reader into closer contact with the personality of the writer.

I owe a great deal to friends and colleagues of Dr. Smart who gave me encouragement and answered my questions; and above all, I must thank Dr. Pickering, the Director of Prison Medical Services, for his sympathetic co-operation; he made it possible for me to visit Wormwood Scrubs and put me in touch with the Medical Staff there and with the Medical Superintendent of Grendon Underwood. I most gratefully acknowledge the kindly help of these members of the Medical Staffs and of the Chief Hospital Officer at Wormwood Scrubs who gave me much useful information. Without their help, this book would have lacked important testimony.

My heartfelt thanks go to the Librarian of the Analytical Psychology Club, Miss Nancy Ralli, who took on the very difficult job of completing Dr. Smart's unfinished book references and collecting all the information for the Glossary: and to Mrs. Dorothea Wallis who not only contributed some valuable comments on Dr. Smart's methods but also undertook the arduous work of compiling the Index.

Finally I want to thank the members of Dr. Smart's family for their help in answering my queries and above all for trusting me with the completion of this work and for so unquestioningly putting all her papers and notebooks at my disposal.

B. Curtis Brown

May 1969.

INTRODUCTION

THIS BOOK IS written from the point of view of a therapist, not of a criminologist, and it is intended primarily for the lay reader who is interested in and would like to know more about the cause and treatment of antisocial behaviour, but who has not necessarily had experience in therapy or in prison work. I have not written it for the specialist: though I would be happy to think that some of my colleagues and others working in the same fields might find interest in it.

My purpose has been to show the possibilities that lie in the psychological treatment of offenders and also to elucidate the psychopathology of antisocial behaviour as this is revealed in long-term investigation and treatment. What has so deeply impressed me in my work among offenders has been the *response* to this type of therapy. Therefore this book is descriptive, not "normative". That is to say, I do not set out to establish a standard and I have made no attempt to be definitive or encyclopaedic.

Ultimately, no problem can be solved by making generalizations and applying universal remedies. In the human field we are dealing with unique individuals for whom no generalization is ever the whole truth. The multifactorial approach is essential. The psychological approach studies the personality of the offender with its unconscious motivations and seeks to find there the roots and origins of his antisocial behaviour. In my own work, the part played by psychological factors is of course weighted, because it is on account of psychological difficulties that prisoners are referred to me: so my interest in the sociological and biological factors lies primarily in the psychological effect which these have had on the individuals I have treated. But in order to give a balanced picture it is necessary to include an account of social and biological etiology, as well as a brief survey of crime study. These will be found in Chapters 1, 3 and 4 and those who are already familiar with this subject-matter may not find anything in these somewhat summary accounts that adds to their knowledge: but readers who are interested in these very important aspects of the cause and treatment of crime will find, I hope, useful references to some of the authoritative statistical work which has been done on them.

My own therapy is based on the psychology of C. G. Jung, but any concept may be applicable to a patient at any time. "Every therapist," wrote Jung, "will ring all the changes that do not figure in his own theory." The concepts of the different schools of depth psychology are often parallel: for instance the infant's experience of a dominating, possessing mother may only need to be interpreted and understood in the terms of the personal mother, or it may have produced a more profound effect which must be interpreted in terms of the archetype. (I will be giving examples of both situations.) So, in treatment, the important thing is to find the explanation *which is valid for the patient*—for his human feelings and reactions—using now this concept and now that one. And there are still other possible interpretations.

The scope of this book is contained within certain limitations, some of which are due to the exigencies of the prison system and some of which arise from the nature of individual psycho-therapy. For instance, in drawing conclusions which would be patent to the reader, we meet one serious difficulty because there is no way of following up a prisoner's progress after he leaves prison. This means that the material we gain from the practice of long-term in-depth treatment of this kind cannot be used statistically. I have based my own conclusions on the changes I have seen during treatment—for instance, the patient's general attitude not only to the doctor but to his fellow-prisoners, the prison officers and his family: his ability to control his emotions, his capacity for making relationships, the change in his attitude to problems outside the prison, such as his relations with his wife or parents or work. Then one can draw important conclusions from any change in his phantasies, especially in the case of a change from homosexuality to hetero-sexuality.

Also, of course, one traces development in the personality from dreams.

Very occasionally a prisoner has kept in touch with me by letter after his discharge: and generally it is reported if a man gets into trouble again and if there is a further sentence and the patient returns for treatment. This, indeed, is very revealing, for it shows what development has taken place in the mean-time.

The validity of all these conclusions of course depends on trusting the prisoner's own statements during treatment. I have found that I can nearly always do so. If they deceive one in their desire to "please" or make a good impression, it rarely deceives one for long—and it is their loss not mine!

Then the number of patients seen by the psychiatrist is very small indeed compared with the total prison population and with offenders in general. The men I see might be called the "cream" of the prison population for they are, in general (though not invariably), more articulate or intelligent and are selected for qualities which would seem to make them responsive to this kind of treatment. Psychopaths and those of subnormal intelligence are not given such treatment—though many of those I treat can appear to be psychopathic in their behaviour. But all the men I see are willing to co-operate—want to help me to help them. Many people think of prisoners as "hardened criminals"—and these no doubt do form a large proportion of the recidivists found in prison. They are men who have adopted crime as a way of life and have no desire to change. The psychological and social causes no longer apply to their problem. These men are not, consequently, suitable for psychotherapy and I must emphasize that these are not the kind of people I write about here.

What I practise for the most part is individual psychotherapy long-term and in depth (and occasionally the time limit of the sentence may make it impossible to come to a conclusion). But not all cases are suitable for this. Some men have little or no capacity for psychological insight and in others the defences may be too strong and should not be broken down.* But with each patient one's approach is on the level that is most helpful and appropriate.

It is for all these reasons—the number of patients who can be treated and the lack of follow-up work on prisoners—the material we gain from the practice of long-term individual psychotherapy cannot be used statistically. There are many statistical reports based on psychological treatment, but the treatment in these cases is often superficial and comparatively brief and it is usually done on large numbers of unselected cases. Some show the part played by social, biological and psychological factors in the general population of prisons, borstals and approved schools. But there have been no general surveys based on deeper investigation—only some studies of individual cases. This is one reason why I felt there was a need for this book, however limited its statistical use might be.

Nevertheless statistical material cannot tell us why, in certain adverse conditions, some boys become delinquent and not

* It is clear from Dr. Smart's reports and notes that even when patients were co-operative in treatment, she often did not recommend continuing psychotherapy if there were factors in the personality which might render dubious results for it. For instance, of a case of Arson arising from "total suppression of sexuality" she reported "at forty-two, it would not be advisable to release his sexual feelings by psychological means, even if possible. ... I consider this man as best left as he is with the determination to avoid getting into trouble in the future." Also see Footnote on p. 32.

others. What counteracts the unfavourable conditions and to what extent?*

In the study of individual cases in greater detail and over a period of time, it is possible to recognize the reciprocal effects of these different factors. We see the total human being reacting to his environment and to his biological constitution, and how this reaction depends on his own unique psychological pattern. As Sir Cyril Burt wrote, "It is the personal reaction to a given situation which makes a man a criminal, not the situation itself."

It takes time, and more doctors than we yet have, to treat all the suitable offenders by the method I am describing here: on a deeper level than can—of necessity—be reached by much of the investigation which has statistical use; or even by group treatment—whose practitioners I much admire and which in so many cases can be helpful. Nevertheless I cannot but feel that the time spent on helping even one individual to become more conscious and better adjusted—and to become, moreover, a better parent—is very much worth while, even though it may be a "specialized" contribution.

From the public point of view, crime is an outrage which attracts attention to a specific event and can—indeed does—distract attention from its real cause. Men go to prison for a specific offence which the Law must take account of in the interests of society. But except in the case of the psychopathic criminal—the man who deliberately chooses crime as a way of life—the offence is not just an isolated event but a manifestation of deep unrest and failure of adaptation. The offender's state of tension has built up over a long time—perhaps over his whole life. From the therapist's view of the patient, it is this condition

---

* The terms "delinquent", "offender" and "criminal" are often used rather indiscriminately—though crime is taken as meaning something more serious than an offence. The term "delinquent" is one used for the young offender: more attention and research has been given to such, because of the possibility of treatment for reform, as opposed to this possibility for the "criminal". Delinquency is likely to have social and psychological causes. But my own experience covers all age-groups.

rather than the crime itself which needs attention: the crime is a symptom. Society needs protection not only against isolated acts but against the psychological condition which produced these acts.

To say this is most emphatically *not* to say that punishment for offences has no part to play. It has an important part, and there are few offenders who do not accept this themselves. If the individual is to achieve a "whole" personality he has to understand what "adaptation" demands, and therefore the need for reparation when a wrong has been committed. The aim of psychotherapy is the repair and restoration of the whole personality, and this means giving the patient a sense of his own responsibility as a human being, and a desire towards the fullest development possible to him.

In the modern world, in which the State has come to be looked upon as the universal provider and society as carrying the responsibility for its members, psychotherapy introduces the concept of individual responsibility and Jung's psychology, I believe, is distinctive in this respect. Facing and integrating the shadow (the dark, unaccepted side of himself) and taking responsibility for himself is often particularly difficult for one whose lack of adaptation has brought him into prison, and it makes great demands on his moral integrity. Nevertheless, though the need is great, so is the response to treatment, and it is this response which makes the work of the psychotherapist so particularly rewarding.

ONE

BRIEF HISTORY OF CRIME STUDY

THE ETIOLOGY of crime has always been a disputed subject and at various times experts have supported different theories about the roots or the causes of criminality. But today the general opinion is that there is, in fact, no one cause of crime; there are many causes, all interrelated, although a single etiological factor may predominate in any individual case. This approach has evolved over the past hundred and fifty years and during this time the emphasis has shifted successively from the social to the biological and the psychological factors.

The conception of a social cause for crime arose during the nineteenth century when the first great social reformers began to expose the appalling conditions under which the poorer classes lived. At this time crime was seen as a social phenomenon arising from conditions such as urbanization—which provided opportunity and anonymity which did not exist in rural areas— lack of suitable employment and bad housing, which led to wandering in the streets. Poverty was an "indirect cause of crime" though "a smaller cause than usually supposed".[1] But even at this period, it was recognized that parental or other adult control was important because it was found that many of the

I

delinquents were boys who had been abandoned by their parents or apprenticed to a master who took no responsibility for them outside their working hours.

At the end of the nineteenth century the Italian psychiatrist and criminologist Lombroso produced a quite different theory of the cause of crime. He turned attention from crime as a social phenomenon to the criminal himself. There was, he said, an unmistakable criminal type of man, who, by a process of atavism, had typical peculiarities of physiognomy of a primitive kind and exhibited primitive emotional characteristics; and he produced a mass of bodily measurements to support his theory. Lombroso's doctrine had very wide international acceptance at the time, perhaps because it appeared to absolve society from all responsibility for the criminal in its midst. But it was not long before his claims were found to be invalid, while the theory itself seemed to threaten the very principle of human freedom by denying the possibility of free-will and responsibility to the offenders.

At the turn of the century, with Freud's discovery that there was an unconscious area of the mind which profoundly affected the emotions and subsequent behaviour, the psychological factor began to be recognized.

In 1909 a psychiatrist was for the first time attached to a juvenile court in the United States. William Healy was director of the Juvenile Psychopathic Institute in Chicago, founded in 1909 with an endowment for five years for the purpose of investigating the etiology and treatment of crime, mainly among young delinquents. In 1915 Healy published a detailed report[2] on his findings based on a study of a thousand "repeated offenders" selected from the total number seen on the basis of "repetition of offence plus sufficiency of data". The average age of the offenders was fifteen to sixteen and he made a speciality of seeing "problem cases". Each case was studied in great detail from every point of view—family and individual history, both social and medical, together with a very thorough physical and psychological examination. Statistical analyses were made of all factors which might stand in "direct logical relationship to delinquency in the individual".

These factors were correlated with information obtained from psycho-analytically oriented interviews in which the delinquent behaviour was traced back to experiences of childhood. Throughout, Healy insisted on the importance of the mental life of the individual, and found that psycho-analytic theory provided him with a key to his study of behaviour. He also found that elucidation of the causes of delinquent behaviour sometimes resulted in cure.

August Aichorn, famous for his pioneer work with delinquent boys in Austria after the First World War,[3] took a number of these boys from refugee camps and organized a special institution for their care. A teacher by profession, he turned to psychoanalysis in his search for an understanding of their behaviour. He came to interpret delinquency in purely psychological terms and had remarkable success in his treatment of these lads.

In 1924, Sir Cyril Burt, in this country, published his standard work *The Young Delinquent*. This was a survey of the social-environmental, physical and psychological factors in two hundred consecutive cases of juvenile delinquency which he compared with four hundred non-delinquents of the same age, the same social class and often living in the same street and going to the same school. He came to these conclusions: a crime is "a mental symptom with a mental origin",[4] and that "it is the personal reaction to a given situation that makes the man a criminal, not the situation itself. It is not bad surroundings alone that create delinquency, but the workings of these bad surroundings on the thoughts and feelings of a susceptible mind".[5]

In 1950 the United Nations instituted a programme for the prevention and treatment of crime and the treatment of offenders. The W.H.O. appointed Dr. Lucien Bovet, a Swiss psychiatrist, to make a special study of the current opinions on the groups of factors relating to the subject, as a contribution to this programme. Dr. Bovet's monograph is a remarkably

thorough and objective work. Carefully examining the relationship between the etiological factors, he writes: "A large
proportion of children and adolescents appearing before the
Courts have no major physical or psychological abnormality.
They are simply the victims of adverse circumstances, characterized by social insecurity or a too low standard of living, or a
combination of both. But for such social factors to cause
delinquency, they must set in motion a number of psychological processes."[6]

This summing up, similar to the conclusions of Burt twenty-
five years earlier, advocates the broad approach which is
generally accepted today. But there are still specialists in each
field who insist on their own particularized view of the etiology
of crime. This is not a disadvantage to the study of the subject
because deeply committed specialists like these promote and
undertake research along their own lines and this usefully
modifies or extends the corpus of knowledge of this many-sided
problem.

TWO

PSYCHOTHERAPY IN PRISON

As was seen in the last chapter, the psychological factor in
crime began to be recognized at the turn of the century. In 1922
Hamblin Smith's *The Psychology of the Criminal* was published
in this country and in the same year, and under his direction,
Grace Pailthorpe began her psycho-analytic investigations in
the Birmingham prison: Sir Cyril Burt was already working
on the psychology of backward and delinquent children. In
1932, a clinic was set up, founded on Pailthorpe's work, which
was carried on by Edward Glover, and organized with
the help of Drs. David Edes, Hadfield and Jensen. This
later became the Institute for the Scientific Treatment of
Delinquency. Glover has written authoritatively on the psychopathology of crime in *Roots of Crime* (1960) and Kate Friedlander
published her *Psycho-analytical Approach to Juvenile Delinquency*
in 1947. While Glover's book draws conclusions which are
extensive and statistical, Friedlander's findings are based
on deep and intensive work and therefore on a smaller
number of individual cases. So there now exists a substantial
amount of literature about the psychopathology of offenders
and also about specific crimes and offences. Here I am
relating my own experiences in working with individual

prisoners to the existing, and for the most part, already accepted theories.

It would not be required of anyone today—as it might have been fifty years ago—to assert the value of such studies in the psychopathology of crime. To take just one example: we cannot over-estimate the value of the work done in disentangling and defining the motive—particularly the unconscious motivation—behind criminal behaviour; and in distinguishing between the "normal", the neurotic and the psychopathic criminal.

Take thieving, for instance. In one form or another this is one of the most common offences. At first sight it might appear to be simply an exaggeration or perversion of the acquisitive instinct, but in fact this is far from being the case. Much more frequently, we realize now, it is a symbolic act—the expression of an unconscious psychological problem. J. R. Rees[7] speaks of the "simple" stealing of apples by the adventurous small boy who wants the apples but is also stimulated by the risk of getting them: this is entirely normal at a certain age. The younger child who has not yet developed a moral sense and has no sense of adventure, simply wants something for itself and expects to be able to have it. Both these attitudes may persist into adult life: the boy's attitude may survive in the car thief or pilferer and the baby's primitive determination in the constitution of the psychopath.

In the context of treatment, there is a wide difference between these two. In the case of the first, in which there is psychological motivation, there is the possibility of treatment: but in the case of the "professional criminal"—the man who *chooses* to live by crime and who is otherwise an apparently normal person—his conduct is not due to any neurosis or psychosis and he does not commit offences as a result of an irresistible compulsion. Such a person has no regrets for what he does: he feels entirely justified because he lives by outwitting other people. These cases are not therefore susceptible—or at least are very much less susceptible—to treatment by psychotherapy.

· · · · ·

When a man is committed to prison he finds himself in an environment which is utterly strange to him. He cannot come and go as he pleases, choose what he will eat and drink, or what time he shall get up or go to bed. Nor does he have to make any decisions about his everyday life and he can take but little responsibility for his family. If he has been in prison before, of course, this environment is not strange to him, but to most ordinary adults the idea of imprisonment has been something quite remote and foreign. I have seen men whose behaviour and personality temporarily underwent a profound change—to the extent, even, of appearing psychotic—on first coming to prison. One young man of twenty-one was given a sentence of ten years for sexual offences against boys. He was allocated to the prison workshops and for about four months the officer in charge could not teach him to do the simplest things: "It's as if there's a blank," he said. I was seeing him at the time and it was clear that this was due to dissociation. The prisoner himself told me later that his mind kept "wandering" to what he was in prison for.

A state of shock like this is, of course, particularly marked among men who have received life sentences for murder. In fact, if there is no evidence of disturbance or distress in such cases, that is in itself significant.

This reaction, however, is not inevitable because in many cases the events leading up to a prison sentence (arrest, trial and so on) have accustomed the offender to the idea of imprisonment: nevertheless for most first offenders a prison sentence means a collapse of their lives and disgrace for themselves and their families. For others, again, it is the culmination and the result of months or years of offending against the law, and for recidivists it may merely be an occupational hazard (though it may still represent yet another failure in life).

The majority of the men and boys who reach the psychiatrist, however, are disturbed and distressed by what has happened and this is an important factor in prognosis and indeed this distress is one of the most important factors in the treatment.

The first offender in this state is likely to be only too glad to have someone to talk to about himself: also he is ready to accept help. On the other hand, to a man who has been in and out of prison all his life in spite of efforts to go straight, psychiatric help will seem like a last desperate hope—and in fact may well be so.

There are still others who seem to take their situation for granted but are willing to give psychotherapy a trial. One man, in whom a dramatic change took place during treatment, said afterwards that he saw it at first as "just another lark". But whatever the initial attitude, there must be a genuine desire to change and a willingness to co-operate if psychotherapy is to be effective.

In my experience, there is a more immediate response to treatment among prisoners than among patients in the world outside: in fact the response is sometimes dramatic. The shock of imprisonment, as I have said, is partly responsible for this. And, paradoxically enough, I have found that the actual circumstances of prison life contribute to the effectiveness of treatment. One of these—the time limit—I consider particularly important. The duration of the treatment is limited to the length of the sentence and after release it is a matter of sink or swim. In general, prisoners are not referred for treatment if their imprisonment is to be less than six months, but I have seen a few cases in which there has been a striking change in an even shorter period. All the same, a longer sentence is generally an advantage in treatment. One man who had two and a half years to do said many times how glad he was that his sentence was no shorter!

Another important factor, which is inherent in prison routine, is that prison makes few demands on the man's sense of responsibility—he cannot make many decisions for himself—and therefore he is not distracted. In itself, this is one of the worst features of prison life and makes the return to normal life particularly difficult. But in the practice of psychotherapy it serves a useful purpose because the prisoner's energy is

8

available to flow into the unconscious. According to Jung, psychic energy is analogous to physical energy and operates according to the same principles of conservation and equivalence. So this withdrawal of energy from the outer world, or extraversion, is likely to lead to a concentration of energy (or libido) in the inner world, that is, introversion. This may result in the activation of unconscious mental processes which can be used, in therapy, to result in a transformation of the personality, that is, to bring about the changes for which the prisoner is seeking. It is well known that if one is totally preoccupied with an outer event or situation, whether with interest, responsibility or anxiety, it is not easy to concentrate on "inner" things, and conversely an individual suffering from a psychosis or even a severe reactive depression cannot attend to outer things. In prison, outer situations such as a marital crisis may hinder the psychotherapeutic process but, on the other hand, the crisis makes it necessary for the man to give attention to this external event and this may mean the widening of his consciousness and a deepening of insight* which also plays its part in the healing process. In other cases, for instance, if aggression has been aroused in the patient himself or has been directed against him by a fellow prisoner, a complex may be activated and thus revealed and this too contributes to therapy.

A prisoner spends a great deal of time alone, locked in his cell.† This is a deplorable condition of prison life and it is due to shortage of staff. But for prisoners who are having psychotherapy, this enforced isolation also contributes to necessary introversion and self-contemplation.‡

Life in a men's prison is tough—and no doubt this is equally true of a women's prison. But this tough masculine world is

---

* Insight in the context of psychiatry, and as used in this book, means, particularly, perception and capacity to examine and understand oneself.

† Many prisoners use this time alone for reading and studying, painting or even learning to play a musical instrument.

‡ An example of this is clearly implied in the statement by "Jerry" on p. 106 (Ed.)

sometimes very helpful, even if hard and difficult, for a man whose masculinity has been over-sheltered by a protective family life. And even a man who is himself tough and hard may come to recognize the value of qualities such as kindness and forbearance against this background. Naturally, this is not to say that prison is a desirable place to be in or that prisons are as good as they should be. Apart from anything else, the opportunity given for prisoners to learn a great deal about crime presents a grave problem. But it can be said that many inherent disadvantages can be turned to useful account by the therapist.

Prisoners are not actually selected for treatment. Under present conditions, it would be impossible for every prisoner to be examined by a psychiatrist and an assessment made of his need and suitability for treatment. This would be an ideal, of course, and we can only hope that it will eventually be realized. As it is, a prisoner's need for treatment is deduced in one of three ways. First, the prisoner himself may request treatment. This is often the case with homosexuals, but it is by no means common, for the majority of prisoners are quite unfamiliar with psychology and psychotherapy and in fact they are often suspicious of it (we all know the slang term "trick-cyclist"!). Prisoners have, nevertheless, become much more aware of the possibility of treatment and of its value during the past few years and requests for treatment are now more frequent. Secondly, psychological treatment may be recommended by the magistrate or judge who passes sentence. This is important and significant in so far as it indicates that the legal profession now accept the fact that crime can in some cases have a psychological basis. Nevertheless, not all cases referred by the Courts are necessarily suitable for treatment. Lastly, a prison Medical Officer or psychologist may recommend treatment if a prisoner has come under his care for any reason. In any case, the initial screening for psychotherapy is always by the Medical Officer in the prisoner's own establishment and there is a final screening by the psychotherapist to whom the man is referred.

The criteria on which the Medical Officer decides that an individual is suitable for psychotherapy, as opposed to treatment by drugs or any other form of physical treatment, are generally known. They are, broadly speaking, intelligence, willingness to co-operate and age. In addition the length of the sentence may be a determining factor. In my experience, the allocation of prisoners for treatment is extremely well based: I rarely get anyone referred to me who cannot be helped in some way. Occasionally a man will change his mind about having the treatment: perhaps because he prefers to return to his local prison so that his family can visit him more easily or perhaps he may find he is unwilling to talk about his personal life. Sometimes treatment is terminated because it is discovered that the motive for seeking it was specious: the prisoner supposed that it would lead to his sentence being served in a prison with better conditions or even to his sentence being reduced. These are total misconceptions! Obviously when such motives came to light, there would no longer be the necessary co-operation and treatment would be ineffective. Again, some prisoners are quite unable to make a relationship with the therapist. This is a feature of the so-called psychopaths for these people have no basic desire to change. Contrary to the assumption, in private and hospital practice, that a capacity for psychological insight is an important criterion for any psychotherapy other than counselling, I find that lack of psychological sophistication is not a disadvantage.

Apart from the presence of a psychoneurosis such as anxiety, obsessional neurosis or depression, the nature of the offence may indicate a personality disorder* of some kind. This is clearly the case in sexual perversion. Arson is considered to be the result of psychological difficulties and larceny may be a compensation for feeling unloved or a means of revenge. An act of aggression may be due to a sudden impulsive outburst of 'untamed' primitive aggression and an otherwise non-aggressive person; or it may be the habitual behaviour of an

* See Glossary.

overtly aggressive personality; or, yet again, the act may be symbolic.

No *class* of prisoner is excluded from the opportunity of receiving psychotherapy if the individual is considered suitable for it, and he will be referred to the therapist who is best suited to his particular needs. Young offenders are obvious candidates, whatever their offence, but older men, including recidivists, may also respond remarkably well.

At the present time psychiatric treatment is given at a number of Borstal Institutions and also at Wakefield Prison where it was begun in 1947, and at Wormwood Scrubs since 1946. Wormwood Scrubs has a well-equipped hospital for all forms of physical and mental treatment where prisoners are sent from all over the country. A psychiatric ward of ten beds was opened in 1946 for the purpose of group therapy and since that time individual and group treatment has been given as well as all forms of physical treatment, including electro-convulsive therapy, drugs and aversion therapy for alcoholics. In 1962, a prison exclusively for the treatment of psychiatric cases was opened at Grendon Underwood, and here research is also being carried out. The opening of this special prison is evidence of the importance which is now given to the psychiatric causes, research and treatment of crime.

The conditions under which psychotherapeutic treatment is carried out are—except that the surroundings are more austere—exactly the same as in private or hospital practice. The patient is seen absolutely alone and in strictest confidence. (Though, personally, I would warn him that if he admitted to some proposed conduct which is contrary to public interest, such as the planning of an escape, I would not condone this.) The limitations of prison life obtain: for instance, if the prisoner is confined to his cell for misconduct he may not be allowed to come for treatment. Above all, it is made clear that treatment can never provide an excuse or cover for punishable offences in prison—nor will it lead to any easing of the term or conditions of imprisonment. Occasionally prison patients want the analyst to make requests for them on their behalf: this is only under-taken by the analyst under very exceptional circumstances, since such requests should come from the prisoners themselves and at their own initiative.

The patients can be treated in a psychiatric ward in the hospital prison if they are disturbed or need special treatment: normally they are seen in ordinary appropriate parts of the prison itself.

As I have said, patients often do not know what the treatment entails—but they almost invariably accept the explanation that it involves understanding the motives of their behaviour, and they understand the point of this. Many naturally have been surprised—and even taken aback—when they have found that they are to talk to a woman, but I have rarely found them unwilling to talk, even at a first interview. Most of them get over their surprise very quickly—and are, in fact, appreciative.

THREE

THE ETIOLOGY OF CRIME:
SOCIAL FACTORS

As we have seen, ever since the early studies made in the last century, it has been recognized that there is a close connection between high incidence of crime and delinquency and the poor social conditions—unemployment, lack of recreational facilities, overcrowding and so on—that exist in parts of the large industrial towns: that is, there exists what is called a "delinquent subculture". These local factors, which operate *outside* the home, I would call "socio-cultural". But these can, of course, be affected by habits and customs—the social mores—of the contemporary national situation. For instance, it has become increasingly common since the last war for adolescents to carry knives, knuckle-dusters and so on, and this in itself facilitates violence.

Within these socio-cultural conditions there exists the more immediate environment—such as the type and quality of the house, the family's standard of living, the degree of squalor or good home organization, the question of whether any of the family have been in trouble with the police, the father's work and habits, the family relationships within the home. These conditions I call "socio-environmental".

All statistical studies have shown that socio-environmental factors are of greater significance than the socio-cultural and, in particular, overcrowding, lack of organization in the home, drunkenness, violence in either parent, the broken home, and above all, lack of love and affection and inconsistent handling of the children. Recent research, notably that of the McCords[8] and the Gluecks[9] in the U.S., has been directed towards correlating and determining the relative significance of these factors. The McCords' research shows that not only is the home atmosphere of the utmost importance—a broken home is a "sign of deep tension and unsatisfying emotional relationships"[10] —but also that loving parents and the type of discipline they impose on the children is of even greater significance and can counter-balance conditions which would otherwise lead to delinquency This detailed correlation of socio-cultural and socio-environmental factors will take us a long way towards understanding why, under similar social conditions, one boy becomes delinquent and another does not.

Socio-cultural and socio-environmental conditions are very closely related and may be interdependent. Poverty, for whatever reason, imposes anxiety and stress on the whole family and particularly on the mother. This results in impatience and irritability and too severe punishment of minor misdeeds. There is also likely to be more parental disharmony—resentment of the wife against the husband and feelings of guilt or inadequacy in the husband which find expression in aggression and violence. Also, overcrowding in the home is a very significant factor in producing aggressive behaviour. These are some of the psychological results of the social factors of poverty in average people who would not be considered neurotic but whose immature behaviour arises from their adverse material circumstances. (The "treatment" here, of course, is the improvement of their social conditions.)

Terence Morris of the London School of Economics[11] has pointed out that the difference in their way of life between poorer and better-class neighbourhoods is also of great importance in determining the patterns of reaction to stress in the children. The middle-class child is brought up in an atmosphere of "controlled care", and is "conditioned to control and restraint from his earliest years; the immediate gratification of desires is discouraged and virtues of thrift and abstinence emphasized". "Sanctions against bad behaviour consists of the threat to withdraw mother love rather than physical violence." In contrast, the working-class child "grows up in an atmosphere in which restraint is often conspicuous for its absence. Punishment and indulgence may follow in swift succession". He "is allowed to develop in relative freedom". Morris also emphasizes the importance of the family as a social unit in middle-class society. It lives as a corporate unit, family holidays being an essential part of life, whereas working-class families may meet as a unit only on occasions like weddings and funerals and the family has less interest in controlling the activities of its members.

In addition, one can often see a difference in the help which the children receive from their parents. Children from very poor backgrounds are often deprived more of guidance in the *constructive* use of their faculties than they are of food and shelter. In the middle-class family, with luck, the child will be shown how to do things or even helped by constructive toys. The slum child may be turned out into the street with no plaything and learning only how to batter and destroy. The frustration of not being able to use his innate skills results in violence and temper.

(To say this is not to say that there is any class monopoly of good parenthood. There are countless "good" mums and dads who bring up their children to be conscientious and self-respecting, persevering and ambitious, thoughtful, decent citizens, and I have seen many cases where one son, perhaps because a particular set of circumstances acted on his personality at a critical time, has got into trouble and the family have been deeply concerned, have tried to understand their responsibility and, above all, have remained loyal to him—even moving to another district to give him a better chance.)

In my opinion, the socio-cultural differences can be significant in determining a child's *susceptibility* to delinquency, but no single factor or group of factors produces the *same* effect on all individuals. Some react to bad social conditions by becoming delinquent, while others (of which there are many historical examples) become social reformers. When we come to examine psychological causes of crime it will be seen that these social and environmental factors are often not *in themselves* the final determinants of behaviour. Ultimately, antisocial behaviour is the reaction of a unique human being to his total situation and this reaction depends finally on the person himself—his basic character and personality.

It is because no single factor or group of factors—however significant statistically—can be taken in isolation that the study of crime is particularly complex.

FOUR

THE ETIOLOGY OF CRIME:
BIOLOGICAL FACTORS

A GREAT DEAL of attention, with much detailed statistical analysis, has been given to the general physical characteristics of delinquents. The results are conflicting. A number of writers have observed that the juvenile delinquent was often of poor physique, undernourished, showing signs of rickets and other nutritional diseases. According to Pearce, juvenile delinquents were found to be less sturdy and robust, were slender, asthenic and with a greater incidence of subnormal nutrition and inferior musculature. These things, he said, "involve increased susceptibility to physical and mental fatigue, and a lessened capacity to compete on equal terms with their neighbours", and so "they reduce the prospect of achieving success and happiness in everyday life".[12] Other writers, however, have seen little if any difference between delinquent and non-delinquent groups. Burt found that "the delinquent as such conforms to no definite physical type" and he goes on to say: "Many delinquent boys are furthered in their violent outbreaks by the fact that their size is not below but above that of their fellows."[13] The Gluecks also found that the delinquents in their groups tended to be superior in gross bodily size and that there was a higher proportion of mesomorphs. Eysenck[14] comments on the predominance amongst delinquents and criminals of *endomorpha* and *mesomorpha*, which supports his view that psychopaths are extreme extraverts. While his statement of observed fact agrees with observations of other workers, this is only a generalization. From my own experience, even, I cannot agree with Professor Eysenck's general thesis that human behaviour is overwhelmingly determined by conditioning. This entirely ignores the reality of the psyche.*

While malnutrition and subnormal physique may in some cases predispose a boy to assert himself through delinquent behaviour, it must be remembered that such a physical condition may well be associated with a poor and neglectful home—which is probably of more significance than the poor physique *per se*.

Antisocial behaviour can in some cases be a reaction to an unfortunate biological characteristic or an accident. A boy who has prominent ears may be the victim of such teasing and ridicule that he becomes a lone wolf and never experiences the security which comes from acceptance by his peers at a time when this kind of identification with his group is essential for his development. He then has to seek satisfaction and self-affirmation in some other way, such as stealing. Deafness or word-blindness may have a similar effect. It is not uncommon to find that the homosexual is of poorly-developed or feminine physique or is secretly deeply ashamed of what he considers to be his small genitals. Sir Norwood East quotes[15] a case of a young man who murdered his sweetheart and then attempted suicide because of his fear of impotence. I myself treated a boy of seventeen, who since the age of five or six had been acutely self-conscious because of his fatness and was consequently unable to mix with other children. He had been in trouble since eleven and at adolescence he was too shy and afraid of ridicule to approach girls, though he felt normal sexual attraction. Another example was a man of twenty-four who, at seventeen,

* See Glossary.

had his nose injured and deformed in a fight. He did not notice the deformity until a year later when a girl made a joke about it. From then on he became acutely self-conscious and depressed; he could not stay in any job and in five years he had five convictions for larceny. While in prison his nose was put right by an operation and this completed the restoration of his self-confidence and he "longed to get back to work". This case was a telling example of the principle that the significant factor is the individual's reaction to his situation. This man needed help for many problems and these problems had interfered with his capacity to deal adequately with his broken nose, but treatment also had to include the repair of his deformity.

There are certain acquired abnormalities of the brain which may predispose to antisocial behaviour. This is very serious if the damage is permanent. Childhood illnesses such as encephalitis lethargica—and, in the past, before antibiotics were available, possibly some cases of meningitis—have been well known to produce such a change in personality. This may also happen after injury to certain parts of the brain. Tumours of the brain, especially in the frontal area, can have the same effect, whether in a child or adult.

A toxic confusional state may give rise to quite uncontrolled and abnormal behaviour. This is familiar in delirium of an acute infection, and it also occurs occasionally in congestive heart failure or renal disease. It is also familiar in alcoholism.

Senility must be mentioned as another cause of aberrant behaviour. Sexual misdemeanours are probably the commonest offences in these cases. (Naturally these unfortunate people are not sent to prison when the cause is recognized.)

Another important biological factor to be considered is the innate mental equipment. Mental backwardness has been considered by some authors to be a contributory factor in delinquency though other workers have found no difference between the intelligence of delinquents and non-delinquents.[16] (It is, however, likely that the more intelligent delinquents manage to avoid detection.) Warren found that the I.Q. of the group he studied varied between 80 and around 140.[17]

This diversity of findings may be partly explained by the fact that years ago no separate provision was made for mentally subnormal offenders—nowadays they are sent to special institutions such as Rampton or Moss Side, in this country. This would exaggerate the importance of low intelligence as a cause of crime.

When it comes to personality traits, there has been general agreement about the characteristic features of delinquents. They tend to have a good deal of drive and to be restless and suspicious, resentful of authority, impatient of frustration and with little self-control. They seek immediate gratification of their desires and therefore cannot persevere so far as to achieve more distant goals. The Gluecks and also Eysenck (as already mentioned) considered them to be extraverted—and indeed their interests are predominantly in the external world—and they certainly tend to lack the capacity to reflect. But there are many introverts among them, as I hope to show in some of my examples. Introversion can, in fact, be a painful condition for young people and they can even adopt an appearance of extraversion to avoid loneliness and perhaps to help them "join the gang".

For many years a more specific personality structure has been recognized, known as the "psychopathic personality". While the behaviour of the psychopath differs from that of the non-psychopathic criminal only in degree, his personality is characterized by two features—a marked inability to have real and lasting affection for others and the absence of guilt feelings. The true psychopath is indeed utterly self-centred, with no concern for the needs of others. He acts on impulse to get what he wants without regard to the consequences, even in spite of his often superior intelligence. He is without loyalty and will exploit his friends for his own ends. He is ruthlessly cruel, and has violent outbursts if thwarted. Sir David Henderson also included in the syndrome of psychopathy a type which he called "inadequate".[18] This type, according to Henderson, is similarly self-centred, immoral and emotionally blunted, but he is passive rather than aggressive. This differentiation, as also that of the "creative psychopath" described by him, has received little support from some more recent authors.

Lastly there are those with congenital constitutional abnormalities. A great deal of research has been done on the association of abnormal electrical activity of the brain with psychopathic personality traits, though it is generally agreed that about 15 per cent of apparently normal people show some disturbance of the electroencephalogram (E.E.G.)* at a single recording. Hill and Watterson were the first in this country to point out the fact that a high proportion of psychopaths had abnormal E.E.G.s (1942). In their series, which they divided into "aggressive" and "inadequate" personalities, they found that there was an electroencephalographic abnormality in 65 per cent of aggressive and 32 per cent of inadequate psychopaths. Investigations since then have shown a range of such abnormality in all psychopaths ranging from around 50 per cent to 75 per cent. Among offenders who are not psychopathic, the incidence of abnormality has been found to be higher than in the normal population.[19] Furthermore, Hill and Watterson also noted that the electrical readings of aggressive psychopaths were similar to those of young children, suggesting a failure of development of the central nervous system (C.N.S.). These findings are of considerable importance in the further understanding of psychopathy (though not of criminal behaviour in non-psychopathic individuals), and especially in the approach to treatment. Clearly psychotherapy is less likely to be helpful where there is a basic constitutional abnormality of function of the C.N.S. In these cases treatment must be

* Discussion of this very technical subject would take us too far from the theme of this book, but those who are interested may refer to some of the many standard text-books on the subject, notably Williams, D. (Ed.), *Modern Trends in Neurology*, London, 1962.

directed towards ameliorating—if possible—the effects of this abnormality.

The relation between abnormal behaviour and epilepsy is far from clear. An association is more likely to exist when the electrical recording is of the type seen in temporal lobe epilepsy. The temporal lobes are concerned with organized feeling and behaviour and therefore abnormal electrical activity in these areas may be manifested in abnormal behaviour and this may be psychopathic. But even if epilepsy is shown to be present, psychopathy may not be the result, but rather another manifestation, of the constitutional abnormality.

I have occasionally had men referred to me in whom more detailed investigation has suggested an abnormality of this kind, which has been confirmed by an E.E.G. Three of these cases are worth quoting as they are all so different. One was a man of thirty-four and his case was very complicated. When he came for treatment he complained of panic attacks since the age of eight; a very violent temper which he knew to be unreasonable but which he was unable to control; dizzy spells for about four years; and heavy drinking since about twenty, as he had found that this relieved the panic attacks. He had had a very unhappy childhood, disturbed by frequent moves. When he was six his brutal and cruel stepfather came home from the forces and he became very timid—"frightened of everything"— and this was not helped by his being put into various orphanages. The family lived in "a terrible area with fighting and drinking". The patient's stepfather was himself a heavy drinker, promiscuous, and a wastrel, and the home was consequently poor and squalid. However, he had a warm and secure relationship with his grandmother and from six onwards he constantly ran away from schools and orphanages to go to her. When he was fourteen she was killed in an air-raid and he became very depressed. For two years he wandered all over the country, maintaining himself by thieving. He had several borstal sentences and a prison sentence, doing many short-term jobs between. He married at twenty-three and had one child but the marriage broke up after five years. After that he tried to get medical help for the attacks of panic and had been in several mental hospitals; but he always discharged himself and then got into further trouble. Finally he was convicted for breaking and entering, for which he received a two years' prison sentence when he was referred for investigation and treatment. An E.E.G. was done and this showed temporal lobe epilepsy.

So in this man's case, socio-cultural, socio-environmental, psychological and biological factors were all involved. The temporal lobe epilepsy called for attention in the first place and fortunately a drug was found which gave him relief from his mental and emotional symptoms. The patient declared: "I feel better than I've felt for years—not worrying about anything." At his own request this man was transferred back to his local prison, so he passed out of my hands. But arrangements were made to enable him to remain under local medical supervision after discharge from prison.

The second case was of a man of forty-two who had had periods of compulsive fire-raising. On the first occasion he was fourteen; he set fire to a large box of waste paper and was put on probation. At twenty-six, when he was working on a farm, he set fire to hay-stacks on two occasions, and lastly at forty, over a period of about eighteen months, he started about eighteen fires in or near the house where he lived. Apart from the first occasion, the fire-raising had always followed fairly heavy drinking. This man had a pleasant, inoffensive personality. His childhood had been happy but he had been rather over-protected and spoilt, being the youngest but one of nine children. His father died when he was four. At ten years old he began masturbating and was told by his headmaster that this would cause blindness. This frightened and horrified him so much that he never masturbated again. Nor did he have sexual phantasies nor overt sexual experiences, though for a short period during adolescence he felt some attraction for girls. But in his own words he "never bothered about sex". Apart from a three year prison sentence for arson at twenty-six his life had gone smoothly and he had had no worries.

This man said he only thought about fire-raising when he was in a particular mood, and this only came on after he had been drinking. The mood was associated with a "tingling sensation down the spine", and he said "Something came over me, something drives me to do it". He would then feel "dizzy and shaking" but once a fire had started he felt "happy and contented". A couple of hours later he would feel guilty, but on the whole he treated it more as a joke. Although he had no conscious sexual feelings, this man himself connected the relief of starting a fire with the relief of sexual tension. The alcohol doubtless removed some of the repressing forces and then sexual tension was released. An E.E.G., however, showed a recording typical of a child of twelve—a type of record often seen in psychopathic persons. This man's socio-cultural and socio-environmental conditions had been favourable. Psychologically he was of a passive rather than an aggressive type and this made him susceptible to maternal protectiveness, and would also account for his reaction of excessive fear towards the head-master's remark. But considering the encephalographic evidence of a basic immaturity of cerebral origin, he had, I consider, done extremely well. When I last saw him he had confidence that he would not find it too difficult to avoid alcohol in the future and this could prevent further trouble.

The third case is a more typical one. He was a youth of nineteen with good and respectable working-class parents and a united family. He was the second of six, the others all being girls. The district where he lived till fifteen was bad, with a good deal of hooliganism, and he often took part in street fights. The home itself was well kept. His childhood was happy and in addition he got a lot of attention from his grandparents. Work was entirely satisfactory. At the age of twelve he had his first sexual experience with a girl, which horrified him and he felt scared, but "it got a habit". From eight years old this lad had transitory black-outs which he described as "coming over funny". From at least five years old he had had a violent temper. As a child he would "shout and scream and throw things". Later he constantly fought with other boys and when roused he lost all control of himself. Yet his personality was kind and considerate and affectionate. The kind of thing that made him lose his temper was the sight of a child being hurt, or somebody being hit! This lad's E.E.G. showed the abnormalities "often seen in habitual aggressives and in a high proportion of delinquents". Again appropriate drugs were found which helped to damp down the violent emotional outbursts so that he was able to control them.

Another important field in the study of congenital predisposition to crime has been revealed only during the present decade—it is that of chromosomal constitution. During their routine studies of chromosome constitution in 1962, Court Brown and his colleagues working in the Clinical Effects of Radiation Research Unit at Edinburgh,[20] noticed that an unusually high proportion of males having an abnormality of the sex chromosomes occurred among the inmates of hospitals for the mentally subnormal who had been *referred there by the Courts*. This casual observation attracted their interest and they have made a special study of the chromosome constitution of males showing mental subnormality and/or behaviour disorders. Casey and his colleagues at Sheffield have been working on the same lines, studying the inmates of Rampton and Moss Side and also Broadmoor.[21] Their findings are identical.

At the present time four types of abnormality of the sex chromosomes are recognized. In one type mental subnormality is the predominant feature, together with a feminine type of physique. In another type there are dangerous, violent or criminal propensities not invariably associated with subnormality. The other two types are characterized by similar behaviour disorders but with a low incidence of mental subnormality. An interesting feature of two of the types is that these men are taller than average. A very important observation made by Forssman and Hambert,[22] and also noted by Casey and his colleagues, is that a significant proportion of these showing abnormalities of the sex chromosomes also have abnormalities of the E.E.G.

This work is only the beginning of important research in this field and we can hope for further elucidation of this complex subject, the genetics of antisocial individuals, in the future.

THE ETIOLOGY OF CRIME: BIOLOGICAL FACTORS

made by Forssman and Hambert,²² and also noted by Casey
and his colleagues. It then a significant proportion of their
abnormalities of the sex chromosomes also have
abnormalities of the I.E.G.

This work is only the beginning of important research in this
field and we can hope for further elucidation of this complex
subject, the genesis of antisocial individuals, in the future.

FIVE

THE ETIOLOGY OF CRIME:
PSYCHOLOGICAL FACTORS

"CRIME IS ESSENTIALLY the solution of personal problems
at a childish level of conduct", wrote an experienced full-time
prison doctor who made a special study of prisoners at Wakefield Prison over a period of about three years, in 1948–51.²³
This comment by Roper, a man whose statements are marked
by their common sense and human approach, corresponds to the
conclusions reached by one of the most highly experienced
psycho-analysts working in a field of delinquency, Kate Friedlander. She wrote: "The antisocial urges met with in delinquents are normal manifestations of the instinctive life of the
small child."²⁴

We are all emotionally immature to some degree in some
areas of our personality but this does not lead us all to antisocial behaviour! Immaturity, however, may lead to this if it
is linked with adverse environmental and biological factors,
and then it shows itself particularly in the realms of aggression
and sexuality.

The normal behaviour of any young baby gives us a familiar
picture of immature behaviour. There is the primitive self-love

which has no concern for others; the instincts are freely and unashamedly expressed, but self-preservation takes precedence over all other instincts at this stage. So the infant's behaviour is determined by the degree to which he feels secure—which at this stage means the degree to which he feels comfortably replete, warm and physically supported.

Freud called this desire for sensuous satisfaction "the pleasure principle". I see it rather as the operation of the instinct of self-preservation. (Later on, when survival no longer depends on such primitive needs, the longing for sensuous pleasure for its own sake can legitimately be called the pleasure principle.) Under favourable conditions it is appropriate for the infant to be passive and dependent. But, in contrast, bodily discomfort, such as hunger or cold, or lack of emotional security, seem to him to threaten his existence and he reacts to the danger in the normal way, with fear and with hostility towards the object which is depriving him. He has not yet learnt to distinguish between permanent and temporary deprivation, so that when he is hungry and cannot have the breast it seems to him as if it were permanently lost and he will die of hunger. He expresses this fear and frustration in the aggressive behaviour we all know so well: the immediate wish must be gratified and postponement is intolerable. If frustration continues the aggression may become quite uncontrollable. This is normal behaviour for the healthy, uninhibited infant but it is *not* normal when it persists into adolescence and adulthood. It is just this persistence of infantile emotions which typifies the aggressive psychopath—only in his case the aggression is expressed through the more dangerous machinery of the adult body and mind.

The emotions experienced by the infant can only be inferred by analogy. But the adult who finds himself behaving like a child may be able to describe his emotional experiences and this provides a valuable source of insight and understanding both for the subject himself and for the therapist.

The emotion that is immediately experienced in a state of

violent aggression is, of course, anger. One patient, a man of twenty-three, said, "The mood dropped into my head and I went flaming mad." When he reflected further on these recurrent moods he recognized that he sometimes felt intensely frustrated and more than once he was overwhelmed by his desire to take revenge. (It was, in fact, an act of revenge that had resulted in his prison sentence.) It was only during his analytical treatment that he came to recognize, first, the hate that lay behind anger, and later, that this hatred was directed against his mother. She was a cold affectionless woman who had rejected him emotionally from the outset so that he—who had, in fact, a warm generous personality—had been severely deprived and frustrated in his longing for love. Here too one could discern the infantile factor of dependence. For when an essential need is not met—and for the infant, love is as essential as food or warmth—satisfaction is constantly being sought for: the very lack of it increases dependence on the individual who should fulfil the need, or on a substitute. But in an adult, dependence creates lack of freedom and this in turn creates resentment and aggression. So this man, who had a driving, restless, extraverted disposition and abundant natural energy, reacted to his frustration and deprivation like an infant—by overt aggression. The fear and insecurity deriving from his mother's rejection showed also in his doubts about his potency— that symbol of total masculine effectiveness: it was significant that his conviction was for rape of a middle-aged woman. Analysis revealed that this act was a symbolic fulfilment of his emotional needs: by this act of rape he experienced union with "the mother", he affirmed his masculinity, and revenged himself by violence.

"The further back in infantile development aggression is traced the more terrifyingly violent and destructive it becomes" writes Storr.[25] The primitive, violent and uncontrollable nature of this man's aggression—which was also often seen during his imprisonment—is a confirmation of Storr's comment. This was indeed a classic case of a man's antisocial activities resulting directly from the immaturity of his aggression. We can see adult aggression, then, as containing the emotions of anger, hate, frustration, fear and dependence.

But childish aggression is not always overt and extraverted. There is a type of child who expresses it in quite the opposite way. One can see some infants who, even from birth, are passive and withdrawn and later on they do not react with the drive and energy of their extraverted brother. This introverted child reacts to danger by flight—by withdrawal. As they get older, these children restrain and contain themselves and express their aggression by silence and non-co-operation. If, later, they become delinquent, their offences are generally committed alone and are often a reaction to their being "unrelated" and out of communication with others (the lack of communication being the result of their own personality). One very introverted and sensitive man I treated, who had had an unhappy and traumatic childhood, had periods of depression when he would steal simply as a form of revenge against people who had treated him badly. Stealing also gave him a feeling of power and exhilaration; and sometimes he stole money in order to "buy friendship". If these children have suffered emotional deprivation they not uncommonly become homo-sexual because they do not have confidence to make friends with the opposite sex. Also they may commit indecent assault or rape and this again is associated with their failure to make a normal heterosexual relationship because of this feeling of unrelatedness.

Sometimes these children escape into a very rich and vivid fantasy world. The value in childhood of an inner fantasy world is described by Frances Wickes, an eminent pupil of C. G. Jung. But, as she points out, the child must progress "from an infantile adaptation to one better suited to a later period of growth".[26] Some offences spring from this tendency to regress into the fantasy world of childhood; when a difficult situation arises there is a compulsive urge "to get away", "to clear out", and a man may steal a bicycle or car to do so. I treated a man of thirty-seven who had often experienced this desire to escape—sometimes it amounted to a dissociation or fugue state in which he was hardly aware of reality and afterwards had no memory of what had happened to him. He was not excessively introverted but had very little drive and self-assertion. An extremely critical father and a dominating, masterful mother had made him feel totally inadequate and as a child he had fantasies of a grandiose nature. Later, when faced with demands he could not meet he would leave home and walk for several days or even two to three weeks, stealing food when he needed it and "sleeping rough". At the end he would find himself in a hospital or a police station, diagnosed as a case of "amnesia".

The attraction of the world of fantasy is not limited to the withdrawn, passive child, however. I had a patient, a young man of twenty-seven, predominately extraverted, who in spite of being happy as a child, had not relinquished the normal fantasies of childhood. His identification with these fantasies led to quite serious offences and imprisonment. When he was twenty-one he was told that he was the illegitimate child of a wealthy woman who had died shortly after his birth. He had been brought up by good and kind foster-parents who were of a more humble class. From the age of twelve—long before he was told the circumstances of his birth—he had inhabited a remarkably consistent and realistic fantasy world peopled by wealthy and attractive "friends", mostly women, who lived normal but romantic lives in a higher social sphere than his own. In his imagination, he eventually married one of them. Because of his close identification with this fantasy world he made friends with women of a higher social class to whom he gave expensive presents which he got by larceny, fraud and false pretences. Eventually his crimes caught up with him and he was sent to prison.*

* This man was well above average intelligence and was distressed by the incongruity of his double life. He co-operated well in his treatment, finally accepting his outer circumstances, with the result

The escapist is certainly immature but this is not to say that he is necessarily weak and inadequate. I have found in these cases that treatment produced increased confidence and that they are ready enough then to face the ordinary difficulties of life without running away. So far as I know, in only one case— and then in exceptional circumstances—did this 'escape' reaction recur.

Nevertheless there are, of course, people who are weak and dependent. Even so, given the necessary support and encouragement in childhood and, in later life, circumstances in which little is demanded of them (and, with luck, a friend or spouse who is willing to give support and take responsibility), these inadequately equipped individuals may live out their lives without serious trouble. But this type can become excessively demanding—and can even end up as the type of psychopath referred to on page 21. This is liable to happen if his parents gave him no understanding and rejected rather than encouraged him in childhood.

Both overt aggression and withdrawal are expressions of the aggressive instinct in the child and normally they are modified with training. But if the aggressive instinct itself is actually repressed it may later break through in a very violent form— even in murder. I once treated a young man of twenty-seven who had been brought up by a harsh foster-mother to whom he reacted with fear and complete submission. Neither at home nor at school nor in his work had he shown any self-assertion or aggression. In course of time he fell in love with his young foster-sister—a hot-tempered self-willed girl who always ridiculed him. One evening shortly before they were to be officially

---

that the fantasy world rapidly faded. After discharge he still liked to associate with cultured and eminent people but was content to do work for which he was suited and which, happily, enabled him to mix with such people. It would have been an extremely interesting exercise to analyse his fantasies in terms of his personality, in addition to recognizing the general compensatory function which they served, but it was not possible to do this since the therapy required withdrawal of his interest from them.

engaged, she began taunting him with what she had got from a wealthy young man whom she had been out with. His hitherto repressed aggression suddenly broke through in an abnormally violent form—he seized a hammer and battered her head with it and she died a day or two later.*

Exaggerated aggressiveness—which is often the cause of criminal behaviour—is generally said to be due to frustration. The earliest frustration, that felt by the young infant, is felt because the infant lacks something it vitally needs. Its aggression then is its response to the apparent threat to its survival. At first, anyway, it is simply a means of self-preservation. Later it may be a reaction to lack of love which, again, is as necessary for the child's emotional wellbeing as milk for its physical health. So even though the instinct of aggression is sometimes transmuted into criminal impulses, aggression as such is a sign of health—certainly as contrasted with the apathy and non-assertiveness which are the mark of despair and inertia.

Jealousy is often expressed through aggression (and most of us have known the murderous feelings it can produce). Considering how familiar it is as a theme in literature and as a phenomenon in ordinary life, curiously little has been written about its psychological mechanisms. Perhaps this is because Freud and the psycho-analysts have attributed it to a persistence of the Oedipus complex and this has been generally accepted. According to Freud, it is first experienced in the child's jealousy of the parent of the same sex and later there may be sibling jealousy— the child's desire to have complete possession of the mother and to exclude his brothers and sisters, which is a derivative of the Oedipus complex.

In 1934, however, J. C. Flugel analysed the components of jealousy in a paper read to the British Sexological Society.[27] He agreed that the emotions experienced in jealousy are derived from the passions felt by the young child towards its parents but he added the rider that the condition of "being in love"

* For the conclusion of this case see p. 100.

produced psychological reactions which engender jealousy. This is because to a person in love, the object of his love is the *only* person who can satisfy him. In the case of a man, "she" represents the "unrealizable ideals of infancy", "the completely satisfactory love object". So if he loses her, his psychological reactions are "greatly in excess of those which a true and purely reasonable estimation of the loss would justify". (He has lost, one might say, not just a pearl of great price, but the only pearl that he recognizes as a pearl!) The loss also produces feelings of inferiority and wounded self-esteem and these are strong elements in jealousy. As Joan Riviere writes, "The jealous person inevitably feels humiliated and inferior, and less consciously, unworthy, depressed and guilty. The explanation of this is that if he is not loved, or thinks he is not, it unconsciously signifies to him that he is *not lovable*, that he is hateful, full of hate. Unconsciously or not, he feels it was because he was not good enough for her and that he has been deserted or neglected by the one he loves. . . . This explains the poignancy and the torturing bitterness of jealousy and this we all endeavour to relieve by condemning and hating someone else, in this case the rival."[28]

Flugel makes the interesting point that there is unconscious envy of the greater freedom shown by the spouse in his wife's aberrant behaviour. He has repressed his own impulses towards unfaithfulness but they tend to break through when he sees them in his spouse. The repressive forces therefore have to be strengthened and this results in more hostility towards the offending partner.

Another cause of excessive jealousy, often associated with paranoid ideas, is repressed homosexuality. The man identifies with his wife and, through her relationship with another man, he vicariously indulges in his own unconscious homosexuality. His jealousy is then reinforced by the fact that the rival shows love for her rather than for himself.

Mowat[29] made a study of sixty-four cases in Broadmoor and found that this paranoid element was the cause of delusions and infidelity—a pathological condition which he speaks of as "morbid" jealousy. These were all cases of psychosis or very severe mental abnormality.

There is one factor not mentioned by psycho-analysts, which I find important in cases involving jealousy. This is the "projection" involved in being "in love" when one projects on to the other person a part of oneself. While there is generally projection of some element of the parent—the "unrealizable ideal of infancy" as Flugel puts it—the loved one also carries the projections of the unconscious contrasexual part of the lover; the feminine part of the man's personality and the masculine part of the woman's (what Jung called the Anima and Animus respectively). When such an important part of the personality is projected the lover feels incomplete and only half of himself when he is separated from the one he loves. When they are together each feels happiness and satisfaction and completion. If we take projection into account, we can recognize that if loss occurs, there must indeed, as Flugel says, be an "excessive reaction" which cannot be estimated by the "purely reasonable" estimate of the loss.

The basic solution in jealousy lies in withdrawing the projection, for then the value which was invested in the other person is taken back in the "projector". It may then be possible to recognize the lost person as an individual in his own right and the lover, instead of denying their goodness and resenting their behaviour, can to some extent become conscious of the value he has projected as being now within himself, and available to him to deploy consciously. This is an extremely difficult thing to do but it makes all the difference between the defeat which jealousy inflicts and the strengthening of the ego and the enrichment of the personality.

Emotional immaturity of the sex instinct is responsible for most sexual offences. Freud[30] expressed the infant's longing for its mother in sexual terms but pointed out that there is also an "innate tendency" to separate from the mother and become an independent individual. He said that normally this begins to take place at the age of about three when the child relinquishes his desire to possess his mother and identifies with his father. But if his love and sexual feelings remain attached to his mother they do not come to the normal heterosexual form that belongs to maturity. In my experience I have found this to be true, not only of homosexuality, but of most of the sexual perversions of psychological origin which are also a sign of immature personality. "Given a healthy development of the whole personality," says Hadfield, "one need not as a rule trouble about a child's sexual life."[31]

The strong fixation to the mother may be the result either of deprivation of love or of excessive indulgence, over-protection and spoiling—when the "mothering" is more a "smothering". In either case the normal masculine characteristics of drive and self-assertion, together with the sexual instinct, do not develop normally. (In the case of a daughter, the effects are varied and differ from those of a boy.)

I have already mentioned (page 31) that very introverted children often have difficulty in establishing relationships with the opposite sex. If this is associated with a mother-fixation the sex instinct will remain at an immature level and these children may become homosexual. On the other hand, the sexual instinct may develop but be inhibited by excessive shyness; then it may be expressed perversely as in rape or exhibitionism.

Many homosexuals have a somewhat feminine physique and according to Hadfield[32] this is due to physiological immaturity rather than femininity itself. Nevertheless, the psychological attitude in these cases is inclined towards the feminine. Throughout my own experience, I have been impressed at the change in young homosexuals that can take place over a period of a year or two while physiological masculine development proceeds; but just the same, the psychological feminine attitude remains. These lads are passive rather than aggressive, anxious to please rather than to assert themselves.

I have found that a high proportion of homosexuals, and particularly immature ones, had been over-protected rather than deprived of love in childhood. This was not due—or not only due—to the mother's behaviour; in quite a number of cases the patient had been the youngest in a family of girls. Sometimes even the grandparents (often so helpful in providing love that is lacking in the parents) have contributed to the spoiling. In these circumstances the father must be very strongly masculine if he is to be effective in balancing the boy's nature!

I have found that seduction by an adult homosexual before puberty, i.e. between about seven to thirteen, is a common phenomenon in the history of homosexuals—not that early seduction *in itself* is the cause of later homosexuality; the emotional basis for this must already have been laid down. But occurring at an age when homosexuality is normal, it may, in a susceptible lad, have a decisive effect in arresting development at that stage.*

Not all cases of homosexuality are an expression of mental abnormality. It may be a biological means of relieving tension, as with animals. The sexual urge (like the other instincts) has a compulsive quality and varies in strength. Consequently in exceptional circumstances, such as a long confinement among members of the same sex, a normal heterosexual individual may indulge in homosexuality for purely biological reasons and relinquish it completely on resuming normal life. He is then simply regressing into early adolescence, when homosexuality is a normal feature.

There are also homosexuals who are constitutionally incapable of heterosexuality due, as far as we know, to endocrine dysfunction. For these people, sexual relations with the opposite sex seem alien and unnatural. Psychological treatment will not

* Homosexual feelings are not abnormal at a certain stage. They may simply represent the identification with the masculine which starts when the child begins to identify with his father at about three years and, later in puberty, identifies with a masculine age-group. In normal cases, these homosexual feelings are "lived out"—though they may not be—and give place to normal heterosexual relations.

change them but it may help them to handle their situation by enabling them to make a better social adaptation.

Rape and sexual assault are aggressive sexual acts. Generally they are committed because the urge cannot be resisted—they are compulsive acts, arising from an unconscious autonomous complex. (The case quoted on pages 30–31 is a good example.) In rape the aggression is specifically directed against the mother. Its very violence bears the stamp of primitiveness and immaturity—gratification must be obtained at all costs and without delay. The act itself is not always spontaneous and unpremeditated but the urge comes up spontaneously and cannot be assuaged. So the act may be planned deliberately in order to relieve the urge. This is particularly true of men whose behaviour is otherwise civilized and respectable.

Exhibitionists, too, are by no means invariably degraded people. Again, the urge to demonstrate their undeniable masculinity to a passing woman or girl is irresistible and sometimes they feel deep shame afterwards. Hadfield[33] has pointed out that at about six to twelve months old it is natural for the infant to call attention to himself by showing off his body, especially when he is being weaned (in which case it is a kind of attempt at self-preservation). In the adult it is likewise a demand for attention—but now it is attention to the sexual potency which he feels to be unrecognized. Again this is an urgent need; for these are men who feel inadequate and inferior because of the attachment to the mother. The urge generally arises at times of stress; and the exhibitionism is a regression into an infantile appeal for attention and support.

Emotional immaturity, as I have said, may be recognized in most delinquents—at least when there is not a biological or a decisive social cause.

But there is another category of adult offenders who are apparently normal people. Sir Norwood East, as a medical officer in the prison service and then for many years director of the prison medical services, had an exceptionally wide experience of prisoners. He found that the majority of the offenders were composed of those whose general behaviour corresponded to that of the average man and that only 20 per cent were mentally abnormal. This percentage is undoubtedly lower than would be found on deeper psychological investigation. Healy and Bronner,[34] for example, treated one hundred and forty-three delinquents referred by the Courts, of whom only 30 per cent were considered on a superficial assessment to be "mentally abnormal". But they did discover that 92 per cent had "major emotional disturbances"—which confirms what many psychiatrists have found, that deep emotional disturbances may only become apparent in the course of treatment. So, as East also said, "the ordinary person is often more potentially criminal than he is willing to believe".[35]

I treated one such case—an apparently normal man—who revealed the potentiality for crime which lies hidden within normality. He was a man of fifty-four, convicted of manslaughter, who came of a respectable middle-class family. His mother "a most wonderful person" died when he was twenty-three, and his father had little interest in him. His childhood was happy and he was, in fact, rather spoilt and pampered by his mother and two elder step-sisters until the age of twelve or thirteen; by then he was an apparently well-adjusted robust boy and got on well at the local school. His ambition was to go into the Navy but he was persuaded against this by his parents and later, when he wanted to emigrate, he was again thwarted. Consequently whatever kind of work he did during his youth was never to his liking. Finally at twenty-eight he did get into work which he enjoyed and apart from six years' war service, he remained in this job and was promoted to a responsible position, with the opportunity to return to it on release from prison. In spite of early spoiling this man's emotional development had apparently taken a normal course. He described himself as "happy-go-lucky", a good mixer, not in the least self-conscious, and "in all the usual scrapes". In his adolescence he had a violent temper and had many fights with other boys,

40

but he was ashamed of his temper and in his mid-twenties learned to control it. Apart from this he was not conspicuously aggressive though he was well able to stand up for himself if he felt he was unjustly treated. He married at twenty-nine and had one daughter. His wife was an incessant talker and grumbler but she was a good mother in spite of her complaints and morbid apprehensions. Since he considered her to be neurotic he tried to behave in a "normal and friendly manner" towards her and to avoid arguments in front of his daughter, even though her behaviour often made him feel "like hitting her or strangling her". For his daughter's sake he did not leave his wife while the girl was young, but by the time he came to prison she was grown up and he had already been planning to do so.

On the night of the crime he went home from work after his evening shift, hoping his wife had gone to bed and was not staying awake to "air her grievances". That morning he had talked with a friend who, over the years, had often irritated him because of his naïvety and weakness. He set out on his usual way home but subsequently remembered nothing of the journey until he found himself at his friend's house, in a state of intense hatred for him and determined to do him harm. He climbed through a window, found his way upstairs, went into the bedroom and attacked his friend with a hammer he had in his pocket, which he had been using at work. The friend's old father rushed in and he struck him too. At that point all his anger left him and he went downstairs and waited for the police to come. The old man died later; the friend recovered.

There are two interesting points in this case. The first is the displacement on to the friend of the suppressed feelings he felt towards his wife which were, in fact, murderous; the second is the dissociation, or "fugue" state, which occurred when he started his journey home and resulted in his arriving at the friend's house without any conscious intention of going there. The very normality of his personality precluded him from even unconsciously accepting a deliberate intention to murder his *wife*; to kill his *friend* was, perhaps, a less heinous offence. But to achieve this, the "murderer within" had to act autonomously, without the full participation of the normal conscious personality. So the conscious personality dissociated itself from the action; he was unaware that he was journeying to his friend's house. The ego, in short, was usurped by the totally alien murderous impulse.

Robert Allerton, whose life story and comments were recorded by his prison visitor, Tony Parker, is another example of the "normal" criminal.[36] Brought up in poverty which he found "soul-destroying and foul and full of shame", he made up his mind that "poverty was not going to be for me". At fifteen after his mother died (she was the only really important person in his life) he was sent to live with an aunt, a heartless, loveless woman, and he soon followed in the delinquent ways of a friend. From then on he chose the life of a professional criminal. Tony Parker describes him: "There were three striking things about him. One was his fundamental lack of desire to go straight, another his refusal to attribute his criminality to outside causes, and the third his critical awareness of his own character. They added up to something I was reluctant to acknowledge because it sounded paradoxical—a well-integrated criminal personality."

East refers to another class of murderer in whom the murderous act is an expression of an exaggerated trait in an otherwise well-adjusted individual: the American lads Leopold and Loeb who kidnapped and murdered a boy of fourteen for no other motive than to commit the "perfect crime". They were well-to-do boys of exceptionally high intelligence. But on reading Leopold's autobiography[37] one is struck, on the one hand, by his lack of moral sense as regards the crime, and on the other, by the valuable work he did for the further education of prisoners during the thirty years he was in prison. The clue lies in his exaggerated self-esteem: in his achievement of the perfect crime he expressed his feeling of omnipotence. His work for his fellow-prisoners would satisfy him for the same reason—producing educational courses and supervising the studies of his fellow-prisoners would give him a privileged position in the prison and he could command the respect both of the officers and of the prisoners.

When we speak of a "normal" person we generally mean one who is well-adapted socially. This adaptation may be perfectly satisfactory under ordinary everyday conditions. But for most people there is a threshold of stress beyond which their social adaptation is likely to break down. As will be seen from some cases I have quoted, this may happen whenever stress builds up and becomes intolerable, as in the case of the man of fifty-four who killed his friend's father: or it may be due to exceptional circumstances such as bad social conditions—or it may be a combination of the two. There are various reactions to excessive stress and antisocial behaviour is only one of them.

On the other hand, there are people like Leopold and Loeb who have certain character traits which, when associated with a lack of social conscience, are likely to lead to crime. It is this lack of social responsibility which differentiates such people from the apparently normal members of society.

SIX

NORMAL DEVELOPMENT

So far i have been dealing with some of the basic psychological characteristics of offenders. But exactly the same characteristics are seen throughout the non-criminal population, and especially in neurotics. So we should, at this point, examine these characteristics in the context of mental abnormality and its origins; and this requires a description of *normal* development and an understanding of some of the terms used in normal psychology.

The centre of the conscious personality is what is called the "ego". When the contents of consciousness at any given moment—such as a memory or thought, or an external object perceived by the senses—are apperceived as such, they are experienced by the ego. In particular, one's sense of individuatily and continuity of identity are related to the ego and therefore Jung speaks of an Ego-complex.*

* Jung introduced the term "feeling-toned autonomous complex", now commonly spoken of simply as "complex". This consists of a nuclear element which is an idea or an object of general experience, together with a number of associations which are charged with emotion to a varying degree. For example, the "mother complex" has as the nuclear element the idea and the personal experience of the mother, and all the associations connected with it, often highly emo-

To the ego belong cognition and conation—that is, intellectual activity, and striving and self-will. If the ego-complex is strong the eruption of emotions ("affects") relating to other complexes can be resisted. A weak ego is easily displaced by another complex and the individual is then overwhelmed by the emotions belonging to that complex. Janet, a French psychiatrist contemporary with Freud, described this as the "abaissement du niveau mental". We see this in everyday life when we lose our temper or when we say "I lost my head". The child is very vulnerable to such inundations because of the weakness of his ego and the strength of his emotions. In the infant these affects come from his primitive and urgent instinctual desires (which Freud called the pleasure-seeking impulses of the Id). Obviously these desires are non-social because they spring entirely from his own needs. But—largely through the relationship with the mother—these impulses are gradually modified and controlled. This growing control further strengthens the ego and contributes to the development of character.

As the child becomes aware of its parents' attitudes and their disapproval of his antisocial instinctual demands, the super-ego or "conscience" begins to develop. The super-ego then supports the ego in controlling the instinctive impulses. At first this occurs only when the parents are there to reinforce it but later the super-ego becomes integrated into the personality and begins to function independently of other people.

So the ego stands between the instinctual demands on the one hand and the moral and ethical standards, represented by the super-ego, on the other. This is the picture of every child's development, provided it is not subject to undue pressures or deprivation. But as we have seen, the delinquent or criminal is generally someone who has not acquired control over his infantile demands, or who deliberately chooses to behave in an antisocial way, and it is important to try and understand why

---

tional, "cluster" around it. Similarly, the "ego complex" is composed of the individual's sense of his own identity, his past experiences, his hopes and ideals, and the emotions he feels about himself.

E

it is that in these cases the balance between the primitive instincts, the ego and the super-ego has not been achieved.
Clearly, those who offend against society must have an ego
which is weaker than the primitive impulses and a super-ego
which is either weak or functioning abnormally: or else, the
instinctual urges are abnormally strong and difficult to control.*

The crucial questions are then: What is the process that enables the instinctual urges to become modified, a strong ego
to develop, and a suitable super-ego to be integrated? What are
the conditions necessary for this? And what are the factors that
interfere with the process? We can only answer these questions
—these fundamental questions—about human nature, satisfactorily, by drawing on material from the wider corpus of
knowledge we now have concerning normal psychology. The
first step is to consider some of the things we have learnt about
instincts.

Instincts are innate dispositions: they predispose us to behave
in a specific way and to experience a specific emotion in relation
to a particular stimulus. Some of these, such as the instinct of
self-preservation, function from birth: they serve the interests of
the individual. Others, such as sex and gregariousness, are also
potentially present from birth but they develop and function
more fully later on: they serve the interests of the group or herd.
The instincts are present throughout the animal world. They
produce patterns of behaviour which are essential for the life of
the species and for each member of the species. So they are felt as
extremely strong urges which cannot be resisted without intolerable feelings of frustration and distress.

Studies of animal behaviour have shown that very specific
outside stimuli are needed to produce instinctual activity. The

---

* Kate Friedlander (*op. cit.*) speaks of the unbalance which leads to
delinquency as "antisocial character formation" which, she says,
"shows the structure of a mind where instinctual urges remain unmodified and therefore appear in great strength; where the Ego, still
under the domination of the pleasure-principle and not supported by
an independent super-ego, is too weak to gain control over the onrush
of demands arising in the Id".

lower the animal in the evolutionary scale of development the more rigid and specific is this relation of outer stimulus to instinctive pattern. Fordham quotes this example from Tinbergen's research. "Directly after birth a baby gull takes up a position immediately below the mother's beak and receives its first feed from her: it is the red spot on the mother gull's beak which evokes the response. Further analysis proves that the red colour is the most important factor."[38] The mechanism by which the suitable stimulus is selected from the perceptual field to release the instinctual response is called the "innate release mechanism". We get other curious examples from Konrad Lorenz;[39] for instance, the "submissive gesture" adopted by a defeated animal which protects it from being killed. This produces an immediate inhibition in the victorious adversary and is absolutely specific for the species. The point we have to notice is that *the outer stimulus evokes the image of the total pattern of behaviour, and this is essential for the instinct to function.* Jung drew attention to this in a paper first published in 1946 when he wrote: "There are, in fact, no amorphous instincts, as every instinct bears in itself the pattern of its situation. Always it fulfils an image, and the image has fixed qualities. . . . If any one of these conditions is lacking, the instinct does not function, because it cannot exist without its total pattern, without its image."[40]

To sum up: the outer objects or total situation activates the inner *a priori* pattern. All forms of instinctive behaviour, then, *are latent in the organism at and before birth.*

But, unlike the animals, the human being has potentialities which are incompatible with the uninhibited gratification of his instincts: hence the need for their modification and control. These potentialities belong to the mental, spiritual and cultural spheres, and can only be fulfilled through relationships with others. "Our civilization is built up," writes Kate Friedlander, "on the assumption that people are able to set their relationship to their fellow human-beings above the gratification of their instinctive desires."[41]

There have been varying views about how and when this

control over the instincts begins to operate. In Freud's view the psychological development of the infant is entirely dominated by the sexual instinct. The development of this instinct is, he says, determined by the pleasurable sensations in each of the erotogenic zones successively: the oral, the anal, and the phallic zones. So healthy progress from one stage to the next will take place only if reasonably satisfactory pleasure is experienced – but not exaggerated – and there is not undue frustration. In other words, each stage must be experienced as fully and normally as possible and without too much psychological or physical trauma. The development and modification of the instincts then corresponds to bodily development.

Melanie Klein's view[42] is that the excessive demand for immediate gratification gives way to moderation when the sensuous enjoyment of the breast is replaced by the awareness of the mother as a person (what she calls "whole-object relationship" as opposed to "part-object relationship"). The infant then wants to please its mother and to win her love—his reward for controlling his primitive emotions. This becomes more important than the immediate gratification of instinctual desires, which he is therefore willing to relinquish. Winnicott says: "What is asked is that the infant shall give up spontaneity in favour of compliance with the needs of those who are caring for the infant."

In later life control of the instincts can be reinforced more or less consciously and deliberately through sublimation; that is, the instinctual activity is replaced by social activity in which it can be expressed and to some extent satisfied. For example, a woman with a strong maternal instinct may take up the care of children, although they are not her own; a creative activity such as writing or painting may be a substitute for sexual creativeness.

Jung has described the way in which among primitive people instinctual energy was transformed into energy for group activities essential for the survival of the tribe, such as war, hunting or work. This was done through ritual ceremonies, as in the spring ceremony of the Wachandi of Australia.[43] "They dig a hole in the ground, oval shape and set about with bushes so that it looks like a woman's genitals. Then they dance around this hole, holding their spears in front of them in imitation of an erect penis. As they dance round, they thrust their spears into the hole, shouting: "Pulli nira, pulli nira, wataka! (not a pit, not a pit, but a c—!). During the ceremony none of the participants is allowed to look at a woman." Jung points out that the hole is analogous to the female genitals and the emotion aroused in the shouting and ecstasy of the dance is sexual emotion. In this way sexual energy is transferred to the earth—the analogue of the original object—"whereby the earth acquires a special psychic value and becomes an object of expectation".

An important point to remember about such rituals and ceremonies is that they are not consciously "invented". They arise spontaneously from the unconscious and their beginnings are lost in the mists of time, before men had sufficient consciousness to think purposefully, and this is why they are so powerful and effective. And as Jung has emphasized the principle of analogy is essential here. The new object must be *analogous* to the earlier one for it to attract the libido.*

* See Glossary.

SEVEN

INNER SOURCES OF CONTROL AND THE CONDITIONS FOR NORMAL DEVELOPMENT

WE HAVE SEEN how strong and compulsive is the operation of the instincts throughout the animal world and, that, since man does not live "by bread alone", he is faced with the task of bringing his instincts under control in order to attain—at least as far as he can—the achievement of his cultural and spiritual potentialities. We may well ask, then, what force is powerful enough to modify and control these compulsive instincts?

A most important factor is the example of the parents—of the adult world as seen by the child. Its influence is indisputable. Not only does the infant imitate adults—as any of us can see if we watch the gestures and expressions of a baby of say, six months old—but if he is in close emotional relationship with them, the young child increasingly assimilates—absorbs into himself—their habits and attitudes.

In technical language, this process is called "introjection" and it starts at a very early age. The initiation of this normal development has been called a "synthetic process"[44] and we could compare it to the "innate tendency" which Kate Friedlander speaks of and to Winnicott's "tendency towards develop-

ment which is innate".[45] Fordham, too, came to the conclusion
that "it was not necessary to impose adaptation on a younger
personality or an unadapted one, because the aim of the
individual or an unadapted person was in any case to do what
other people did, i.e. his natural aim was to become normal and
adapted".[46]

This innate tendency to develop beyond the sheer exercise
of the instincts is seen particularly—and often very impressively
—during the treatment of disturbed people, in whom the normal
process of development has been interfered with: where conditions have not been "good enough" to allow it to proceed.
Without it therapy could not be effective.

This tendency towards wholeness and development was
recognized by Jung as proceeding from a specific centre of the
personality. He called this centre the "Self". This concept of the
Self is highly important and to understand it requires some
knowledge of Jung's concept of the unconscious. I will be dealing with this later on, but at this point it may be enough to say
that the total personality consists of consciousness (the ego), the
Personal unconscious and the Collective unconscious. In Freud's
view the unconscious was purely personal—the repository of the
forgotten and repressed contents of consciousness.* But Jung's
view is wider. He held that the personal unconscious contained
not only repressed material, but also the unlived potentiality of
the individual, both good and bad, and it rests upon a deeper
layer, which does not derive from personal experience but is
inborn. This deeper layer is the Collective unconscious for it
contains "all those psychic contents which are peculiar not to
one individual but to many at the same time, i.e. either to a
society, a people or to mankind in general". These "contents"
he called Archetypes (a name he borrowed from St. Augustine)
and they manifest themselves as universal images that have
existed in the human race ever since the remotest times.[47]

It is to this lower layer of the unconscious that the instincts

* Freud came later to admit the existence of a racial unconscious but he
gave it far less importance than did Jung.

also belong, because they, like the archetypes, are inherited and occur uniformly and regularly in all members of the human race.[48] But while the instincts give rise to certain typical forms of behaviour, the archetypes determine our apprehension of events. As images they occur in dreams, in the hallucination of schizophrenics and—collectively—they are the stuff of myths and fairy tales. They have been given expression, too, by creative artists throughout the ages.

In the course of his work with adults, Jung was led to the conclusion that this three-fold totality of the Conscious, the Personal unconscious and the Collective unconscious—the "centre" of which is the Self—was the source of the urge towards wholeness of the personality, that is, the source of the tendency towards development. But development is concerned not only with the modification of the instincts; it includes also the emergence of the ego—the conscious mind—in infancy and the maturing of the ego in childhood and throughout life.

Jung reached these conclusions as early as 1923: more recently Fordham, in his studies of children, has brought evidence to confirm them. He too, sees the "self" as the original archetype in infancy and the conscious mind emerging from it. And as consciousness arises in the young infant, he says, there is a readiness to perceive and act, but there is, as yet, no perception or action. "Both come with consciousness together with that distinction between subject or object. . . . We assume that only when the object fits . . . can a correct perception occur. . . . Thus small children *need* objects, whether they be parts of themselves or parts of others. Through these objects, it seems that the child's consciousness of himself as a whole person grows . . . as does his image of other persons as whole beings."[49]

This gives us an interesting parallel with the operation of the instincts: outside activation of ideas based on pre-existing and unconscious archetypes lead the infant to develop conscious response and action, just as outer stimuli activate instinctive behaviour. And both—perception and apprehension on the one hand, instinctive behaviour on the other—derive from the unconscious and are necessary for developing the ego to meet the demands of life in a human world.

Normal development, then, is initiated by the Self, but even so there must be certain minimum conditions in the environment if the ego is to develop—if the infant is to become a "whole" person. There must be the "good enough" conditions Winnicott spoke of. The most important of these is love. Love belongs to universal human experience and everyone has his own ideas about it. I want only to describe the aspects of love that are important for the child's development.

For the infant, the mother and her breast are his entire world.* At this stage he must have security and containment, both physical and psychological, and he is dependent on his mother for every need. He is also at the mercy of his own emotions. So security and insecurity are precariously balanced, and to keep fear and frustration at bay, his mother must give him not only food and warmth—his physical needs—but also the support and comfort of love. When she meets both these requirements she protects her baby from excessive anxiety and from his own violent emotions which arise from his primitive instincts of fear, anger, frustration and hate. For a baby, these emotions are felt as something very dangerous inside him, threatening his very existence. One has only to see a very young infant in violent paroxysms of crying to understand the fear that such uncontrollable emotion must produce. *He* cannot control or contain it: only his mother's stability and strength can give him security.[50] The strong, quiet, loving mother who can tolerate her baby's noisy violence will help to lay the foundation of a personality whose aggression is ultimately controlled by the ego, and who will be self-affirming rather than aggressive towards other people and towards society when he becomes a man.

But besides being a bulwark against the dangers that seem

---

* Later on the father and siblings are important for him, but at this stage the importance of the father lies in the mother's relationship with him. This will be reflected in her attitude to the baby.

to threaten him from outside and inside, the mother acts as a mediator in the child's experience of the external world, and this too affects his attitudes in later life. If he feels loved and accepted he will be more likely, later on, to be confident that people are kind and well-disposed towards him—far less likely to carry a chip on his shoulder and invite hostility by his own defensive behaviour. As the infant comes to recognize his mother as a person (that is, to have "whole-object relationship") and feels her love for him and his for her, he begins to want to please her. Hostility towards her feels like a kind of destructiveness which may destroy her. This gives him his first sense of guilt and he longs to make reparation.[51] This is the beginning of a social conscience: the hitherto absorbing self-love is diminished by concern for another person.

Now we are coming to the stage where restraint and control are needed. A healthy infant very soon shows self-will based, of course, on his primitive desires (which can now appropriately be called by Freud's term "the pleasure principle"). Indulgence is no longer always helpful to him here. Limits have to be set; a certain amount of discipline imposed. This again produces frustration, with its anger and hate. Nevertheless, the child feels much more secure when he knows that there are firm and consistent limits to his demands. He cannot set these for himself and if they are not there to make a safe outer framework, he is back again at the mercy of his own violent emotions. Now it is the ego which is being supported against the primitive instincts. He has to learn to relinquish these and adapt his behaviour to social demands. In the course of time he absorbs—or integrates—this outer discipline into himself and imposes it upon himself: so the instinctual impulses are brought under his own control and we get the super-ego, or conscience, beginning to develop.

At this point the father plays an important part. He represents authority and if he exerts authority with kindness and understanding he will give further security to the child against his violent impulses.

54

From the very beginning, a child identifies himself with his parents. "Good" parents will help immeasurably to build the child's ideal image of himself—what is called his "ego-ideal"—and their moral and social standards will help to form a strong but tolerant super-ego.

An extreme example of the way that early conditioning affects the adult and his society is given by Margaret Mead, the social anthropologist, in her study of two primitive societies.[52] In one of these communities, the infants are nurtured in uninterrupted close physical and psychological contact with their mothers: there is no separation or sudden weaning, and so they are protected from any anxiety or insecurity. These children develop into contented, secure—if passive—people. This is characteristic of their culture, where social relationships are almost entirely free from rivalry, hostility or any other a-social aggressiveness. In the other community, the children are deliberately subjected to disturbing experiences and they develop strong antisocial aggressive qualities, such as anger, violence, and ruthless competitiveness: for in this community these traits are considered admirable.

But the aspect of love which I have found to have the greatest importance in later life (and includes what has already been described) is respect for the child's personality. From birth onwards, the infant is an individual in his own right—the mother already knows something of this from the movements she has felt in her uterus before it is born. The handling of the child, both physically and psychologically, must be relaxed and untense—which means that it should, as far as possible, allow him free expression of his personality. Again, the shy, introverted child cannot be pushed into being as sociable and outgoing as the extravert. This kind of child needs to feel accepted as he is: if anyone tries to force him into extraverted behaviour he will withdraw still further. Similarly, his more aggressive, restless brother needs help in finding an outlet for his energy: otherwise he becomes violent and destructive. Whatever his type of personality, a child needs to feel loved and accepted *for what he is*—which is sometimes difficult for parents because they often have an ideal image for their child and cannot resist trying to impose it on him. But this, which is a violation of the child's own intrinsic personality, will burden him with problems in later life.

So the right kind of love is the basic condition for normal development because this enables a child to gain control over his primitive instincts, to modify them so that they are made available for constructive use by his ego. It gives him confidence in his own personality, so that he grows up rooted in his true self, and it gives him a framework of social behaviour within which he can express himself without violating social obligations. The basis is laid down for the integrated and well-adapted individual—what Wordsworth described as "The Happy Warrior".

Such an individual will be more able to resist the pressures and temptations of adverse circumstances, such as unfavourable social conditions, or unavoidable misfortunes—such as physical or emotional vicissitudes in his personal life, which can have a devastating effect on someone with a less secure childhood behind them. (For example, later separation from one or both parents can be borne without too great harm.)

And here we should look at another important condition for normal development—a stable family life.[53] The relationship between the parents themselves is important in two ways. First, in the security a child gets from a relationship in which there is love, co-operation and a united attitude to life and the family. The child's life is set within the environment of the home and family and if this is threatened with disruption it means disruption of his entire world. Secondly, the parents represent for the child the masculine and feminine principles. We all carry within us the rudiments of the opposite sex, both physical and psychological. But the generally accepted relation between the sexes is that the male shall be the stronger and more dominant and that the female will be willing to accept this domination. If something of this balance exists between husband and wife, the boy or girl gets a clear image of the relation of each sex to the other on which he (or she) can unconsciously model his attitude to the opposite sex. Moreover, the relationship between the masculine and feminine which he sees in his parents will determine the balance between masculine and feminine qualities in his own personality and this too will affect the development and functioning of his instincts. (This point will be dealt with later on.)

Finally, in this survey of the parents' role, there is the question of the consistency of punishment. This was touched on in the chapter on socio-environmental factors, but it is so important that it is worth enlarging on here. A child has to "test out" how far his primitive aggression is tolerated in the outside world and discover the limits of this tolerance. If punishment and reward are inconsistent he will be uncertain about these limits. This will give him a feeling of insecurity about himself—he will not know "how far" he can go. If this has not been made clear in the home he may have to do this testing out later on in the outside world when it will take the form of delinquent behaviour. His behaviour is then really an appeal for the strong and consistent authority of a good father figure. We have ample evidence to show that consistency of discipline bulks very large in the prevention of delinquency: this is true even if the discipline is harsh or even brutal. When the McCords[54] correlated this factor with others, such as parental love and cohesiveness of the home, it was shown to be decisive even under otherwise unfavourable conditions. What is more, consistent punishment and reward establish a code of values and a standard of behaviour which give the child a basis of confidence even if he modifies this later in accordance with his own individual development.

As the child grows older others, as well as the parents, of course, play a part in his development; for instance, in his immediate home life, his relation with his siblings becomes important. According to Alfred Adler, the position of a child in the family produces its characteristic effects. The eldest may be conditioned to being treated as an authority by his younger brothers and sisters and this may develop in him a feeling of

57

superiority: or, in some cases, the sense of responsibility may overburden him. The youngest child may be petted and treated as the baby, become overdependent and unable to trust his own judgements because others "know better". There is plenty of room for these variations within normal developments. Nevertheless they may determine tendencies in the child's ultimate character-formation.

Later, when he goes to school, he has his first initiation into the outside world where he no longer gets the protective love of his parents but finds himself standing alone as himself. It is now that the confidence given him by wise and helpful parents is put to the test: and he will meet new figures of authority who will again affect his attitude to authority. His intrinsic characteristics will begin to show in his relations with his own age-group—whether he is aggressive and bullying or retiring and submissive or independent. Meantime the restraints of discipline he learnt at home continue.

Apart from home and school influences there are socio-cultural conditions of the neighbourhood which play a part in development; and these too will test the quality of the home background and his own personality. The importance of this socio-cultural environment in the causation of crime was dealt within in Chapter 3, but it has a special psychological significance also. At adolescence, separation from the parents is part of normal development: the normal step at this point is towards identification with his age-group, through the membership of a gang or a club or through boarding-school life. By now the super-ego has been established according to the pattern of the parents' standards. But in the need to become an independent personality, this pattern may be displaced by that of the social group. So the nature and mores of the group may have a disproportionate influence on his development.[55]

We are all sensitive to the approval and admiration of our fellows, particularly of those whom we admire and want to emulate and the adolescent is, at least temporarily, deeply influenced by the standards of behaviour of the group he is identified with. But he is less likely to be influenced to act against his will if he has developed a strong ego and super-ego through early *consistent* discipline.

I have not attempted here to cover all the factors that might contribute to normal development of personality, only to indicate the essential part played by love and care in early childhood. In the next chapter I shall describe some cases in which there had been serious interference with normal development.

EIGHT

FACTORS WHICH INTERFERE WITH NORMAL DEVELOPMENT

THE GREAT MAJORITY of the men and boys whom I see in prison have parents who were neglectful, rejecting, actively cruel, over-possessive or dominating: or they have lost one or both parents in childhood. In short, they had been deprived of the kind of love necessary for normal development. As will be seen, I have differentiated between actual lack of love, such as rejection, and "faulty" love, which includes possessiveness, domination and over-protection. The mothers who fall into the latter category—and it is generally the mother—are those who are concerned about their child's welfare and are generally well-meaning, but for various reasons (such as their own complexes) they damage their child's development.

There are other cases, of which I have met several examples, in which a lad exhibits delinquent behaviour for no apparent reason at all, the family being a cohesive one and the parents wise and sensible. Some of these cases I could only attribute to something apparently unimportant, acting on an exceptionally susceptible personality. For it must be remembered that the *most important factor is the personality of the victim of adverse circum-*

stances and "the working of bad surroundings on the thoughts and feelings of a susceptible mind".[56]

One very disturbing example of rejection (there were here, as always, other factors too) was a young man of twenty whom I shall call Martin. He complained of many problems and of being "completely mixed up". His symptom was depression in which guilt feelings were very marked. He had suffered from this since he was thirteen and had taken amphetamine drugs to relieve it for two years before I saw him. He also had an obsessional anxiety about dying, and this was associated with a phobia for fire, which for him suggested hell-fire. As a child he used to lie in bed in a sweat, thinking his last moment had come. He had physical symptoms of anxiety such as palpitations and difficulty in swallowing, and he often thought he had a tumour in his chest or head. He was afraid to sleep in a strange bed in case anyone had died in it. When he looked at himself in a mirror he saw himself "as if dead". While in prison he had dreams of death or mutilation, such as being hanged, or of people being "ripped in half".

Martin's mother was, according to his account, very immature. She had been unwilling to bear him. She did nothing in the house and each time she became pregnant she took drugs to produce an abortion. In two pregnancies after his birth (one of which resulted in twins) the babies were born dead so that he was virtually an only child. His wife told me that his mother showed no love for him and said she wished he had died like the other babies. The mother herself was obsessed with illness and dying: she was convinced there was a "death-watch beetle" in one of the rooms of the house they lived in, and constantly spoke about it. Nevertheless the patient was—on the conscious level—very fond of her.

His father had sinister associations for him. He had not worked since the First World War and died when Martin was fourteen. He had a mental disturbance for which he had to go into hospital for up to six months, once or twice a year. When Martin was between the ages of eight and eleven his father showed a homosexual interest in him, though there was no actual homo-sexual activity. He had a violent temper, which made the boy anxious; but they were fond of each other. The father did the housework, cooked and looked after his son, but the home was extremely dilapidated. Martin's description of home was a dirty room with "the paper filthy and peeling, no light shades, the chimney smoking because it was never cleaned, and Dad sitting there all scruffy and dirty. I could see him there through the smoke looking really mad, especially when something upset him." The whole atmosphere was scaring like films of people in haunted houses. Most of the time he was scared of his parents – "mother's staring eyes and father smashing windows" (when his father's mental illness was coming on). Normal play with other children could not counter-balance all this as up to the age of thirteen he was kept strictly at home. There was, however, a kind and affectionate godmother with whom he spent happy week-ends—the only place where he was happy.

This man had been introduced to homosexual activities at seven years old and from the age of fourteen he earned money as a homosexual prostitute (when he was not in an approved school, remand home or borstal home for breaking and larceny). But in spite of all this he fell in love with a girl with whom he had completely satisfactory sexual relations and whom he married.

Martin had never felt any great hostility towards his mother and in fact he had a horror of violence. During his treatment, (which was only for the last eight months of his year in prison) his aggression began to emerge. Later, after he left prison, it got released under the influence of drugs. A few months after his discharge he murdered an old woman in her home and was com-mitted to a criminal mental institution.

The most striking thing about this man was his obsession with death. I could not avoid the conclusion that this was associated with his mother's early rejection of him and her active efforts to destroy him while still in the womb. Death then was literally an imminent danger. That, in fact, he did have violently destructive death-wishes towards her was confirmed by his fear of violence, followed by his own act of violence against a mother figure.

His previous delinquent behaviour was the result of being involved with others rather than through his own wish. Social factors had largely determined the kind of people he mixed with and they were delinquents. In addition he had an identification with his mother which made him an easy prey for homosexuals and, suffering from depression, he began taking drugs. He had had innumerable jobs but never persisted in any of them—he lacked perseverance. Every circumstance in his childhood had prevented the ego from being strong and consequently it was at the mercy of both his outer environment and the inner fears of his own destructiveness. The super-ego was, of course, similarly weak and vacillating. Even so, there was in this man a basis of the super-ego which was reflected in the depression and anxiety and in the strong feelings of guilt which rose from the repressed aggression. It is possible (in theory at least) that a sufficiently long and deep analysis might have modified Martin's personality, especially as he was very anxious to have treatment and could have co-operated extremely well. But this is doubtful because the damaging rejection took place at such an early stage.

What was remarkable was that he had warm feelings and a capacity for relatedness. Under such adverse emotional—as well as social—conditions one could have expected him to be a psychopath, with a typical lack of any humanity in his relationships and with no sense of guilt or shame—let alone anxiety or depression. I think this could be attributed partly to the affectionate relationship with his godmother. Also, his mother was not quite indifferent to him: he said she was more like a sister—so that although she rejected him as a son there was some emotional tie with him, even if hate was a component of it.

Often a stepmother can make a child feel severely rejected. Harry was a young man of fifteen whose mother had deserted the home a few days after he was born because her husband was having an affair with another woman whom he later married. The father was a hard man and a heavy drinker[57] and Harry and his brother came in for many beltings. He had been in prison himself and taught his sons to steal; so they had no love or respect for him. The stepmother showed no affection whatever, pushed the boy out into the street to play and neglected his clothes, food and cleanliness. When he was five years old he was evacuated and was quite happy in his temporary home, but at eight, after he had returned, he was sent to a children's home and from then until fifteen he was at various children's homes and foster homes and finally an approved school. This repeated shifting about from one environment to another increased the feeling of rejection and insecurity and made it more and more difficult for him to form lasting relationships. In prison he asked for treatment on account of homosexuality with boys of ten to twelve. He was very cut off from his feelings—he trusted no one and suspected the motives of anyone who showed him kindness. In practice, he disliked and suspected women because, he said, of the way his mother and stepmother had treated him. But he had compassion for children and vaguely wanted to work with children. He recognized that this was a desire to help the unhappy child in himself. During the course of six months' treatment he began to have heterosexual phantasies and became confident that he would be able to relinquish the desire for boys. His friendliness with other prisoners increased and he became more hopeful about life. But apart from the sexual development, I could not feel very sure that there could be any change in personality in so short a time. (I have not heard anything about him since his discharge.)

Stealing is a common reaction to feeling unloved: the stolen objects being a compensation for the missing love. In themselves they may be quite superfluous and unwanted—they may even be thrown away—or they may be stolen to give to others in an attempt to "buy love and friendship". In one case I had, the boy only stole from members of his family; he was expressing his revenge and also calling attention to himself.

The feeling of rejection can be associated with jealousy of a brother or sister whom the parents seem to prefer. Sometimes if there is derision and ridicule and comparisons are made, the child has to overcome feelings of misery—his inferiority, frustration and anger—by having to be "big" and draw attention to himself by actions which compensate him and revenge him on his parents. Sometimes he can only feel accepted by associating with a gang and earning their respect and admiration by joining in their delinquent activities.

On the other hand, a mother's "faulty love" interferes more often with the sex instinct—though this does not invariably happen. A dominating, possessive or over-protective woman is likely to be married to a man weaker than herself and if so, the mother rather than the father is associated with domination and strength. When he is about three years old, the child should relinquish his longing for his mother and identify with his father.* But if this normal tendency towards development is checked in the child because his mother is unwilling to let him grow up in this way and he is not supported by a strong and encouraging father, he will remain fixated to his mother and will identify with her instead of his father. He may then fail to develop his normal masculine sexuality. As we have seen, homosexuality is the commonest manifestation of this situation, but indecent assault (on either sex), rape and exhibitionism can also result from it.

Another very serious cause of damage comes from mothers who are themselves unsatisfied and who seek for satisfaction in their sons. A mother may even go so far as to seduce the boy when he is adolescent; more often, she lets him—or takes him—to sleep in her bed. This physical contact can produce personality problems which are invariably deep and difficult to treat. (This taking into bed is not for a moment to be confused with the normal cuddling of a loving mother who lets her child come into bed with her, when in the course of play he feels and

* This is the normal solution to the Oedipus situation.

enjoys her body. This does not spring from the mother's need for emotional fulfilment but for the fulfilment of her maternal instinct.)

Eddie, who had this childhood experience, was a young man of twenty-one whom I treated. He was psychopathic, sadistic and obsessed with fire: he had committed acts of arson. He had many dreams and fantasies of killing his mother and burning her house down and he had also had auditory hallucinations since childhood. He was finally committed to a criminal mental institution. Another, Frank, a boy of eighteen, a homosexual, had the added disadvantage of having three older sisters who all spoilt him. He was a schizophrenic. He responded to physical treatment in a mental hospital and then to psychotherapy in prison. It is interesting that these two seriously disturbed men had auditory hallucinations, for this indicates a serious dissociation, or splitting, of the personality.

Eddie, the psychopath, slept in his mother's bed, when he was seven to ten years old and much later he suspected that his mother wanted to seduce him. The auditory hallucinations began at fifteen and continued. There was one voice, always the same, which told him to attack his mother (which he had done on one occasion) and other people who bore some resemblance to her. In the case of Frank, the schizophrenic, the voices urged him to kill his earlier homosexual friends and also the homosexuals in prison: and he had actually tried to kill the boys he knew outside on more than one occasion. He admitted to his hatred of his homosexuality and the hallucinations were the manifestation of his desire to kill the homosexual part of himself.

It would be wrong to assume that the mother's overt advances, in these cases, were the *direct* cause of the serious personality disturbance, for the psychotherapy included the total relationship to the mother. The fact that a mother seeks emotional satisfaction in this way indicates the seriousness of her own psychological difficulties and these in themselves are likely to affect a vulnerable son from a very early age and to lay the foundations for his susceptibility to any abnormal stimulus later on.

In any case, it seems that the form that the symptoms took was affected—if not determined—by the abnormal relationship. But there were other factors operating; in each of these two serious cases, the father took no interest in his son and so gave no masculine support.

My third example is different. This was George, a lad of twenty-two, who, basically, had a good personality. His sexual development was normal; he had done well at school and in work and in the R.A.F.; he was above average intelligence and had good insight. And all this in spite of the fact that, in addition to having an unstable mother, he had a father whose only interests were women and drink: his relations with his wife were bad and he beat the boy frequently. The boy's mother had little interest in him after he was about thirteen, but when he was eleven she liked to have him in bed with her (her husband had left home some eight years previously). This boy, too, had auditory hallucinations. They started at the time when his mother was taking him into her bed and had persisted ever since. They were the voices of numerous young boys telling him to do destructive things and he was unable to resist them. For example, they told him to damage his eyes and he had tried to do this; to steal—and this had brought him to prison. They also told him to kill his mother, which he had attempted to do, though unsuccessfully. He complained that he had a violent and uncontrollable temper when he was thwarted. The hallucinations indicated a splitting of the immature aggressive instinct which had, presumably, become violently activated when his mother became a serious threat to his normal sexual development. But, in spite of his mother's instability, he was fond of her and she looked after him quite well until she remarried when he was fourteen. This accounts for his being able to develop a basically good personality. Also he had a good relationship with each of his grandfathers, who would therefore have compensated to some extent for his father's lack of affection and support.

These are extreme cases in which actually unnatural demands

have been made on a son. But many mothers are simply dominating, possessive and over-protective. This is the history most commonly found in cases of any kind of sexual perversion. The over-dominating influence of the mother, even in her feminine role, one must remember, is in ratio to the influence of the father. The father may be merely uninterested in his son, but he will then fail to exert authority and his son will not respect him nor try to emulate him. He may, in addition, be at the pub or football match more often than at home. Or he may drink, in which case his home-coming may be dreaded, and if he is also violent and brutal he will be hated, feared, and despised. In none of these cases will the growing boy identify with a strong and admired masculine figure and he will be likely to keep an over-emotional attachment to the mother even though she may not be an unduly dominating personality.

I had a particularly striking example of this in Cox, a man of thirty-seven. He came from a respectable middle-class home. The mother was evidently a very feminine woman; Cox's wife said, "She was very gentle but strong. She wasn't possessive—she welcomed me when I married her son." Mrs. Cox said also that her husband was "devoted to his mother and was never critical of her. He meant everything to her too, and his personality was very like hers". But the mother was somewhat prudish and pious as well as over-protective, and she lacked the toughness to help her son to face the masculine world. The father had a violent temper, drank heavily and was sometimes cruel, even brutal, to his wife and son. He also had homosexual tendencies and exhibited himself to his son when he was a small boy. The mother showed obvious preference for the son, which the father naturally resented. He ridiculed and belittled the boy in front of people. (A daughter had died in childhood before the boy was born; the father idolized this child and did not want a son.) The boy idolized his mother and hated his father. The result was that he had a strong identification with the feminine, and his personality showed this. He was gentle and kind and had artistic and aesthetic tastes. While in prison he worked as an orderly in the hospital, happily and successfully, for the work called on his particular qualities. He was an active homosexual, though he was married and had two children. (It was for a homosexual offence that he had been sentenced and he asked for treatment in prison.)

Here was a case of a man who might well have been normally heterosexual if his early background had been different. The first year of marriage was very happy, largely through his wife's helpfulness. Then he began to feel that he was "using her" and held back, letting her take the initiative. Then he lost interest and began to seek male company once more. It seems clear that heterosexuality was associated with guilt feelings because as women were identified with his mother, they were too pure and holy to be "used" for sexual pleasure. In other words, the super-ego was based on the rigidly pious standards of his mother, in which sex, sensuality and physical toughness were disparaged. In this case, the antagonism between father and son interfered with the integrating of masculine ideals with masculine behaviour while the idealization of his mother resulted in his identifying himself with standards which were inappropriate for his masculine development. This man did, in fact, suffer from severe depression and anxiety showing that the development imposed on him was fundamentally opposed to his own nature.

I have treated several men whose confidence had been damaged by an over-critical father ("my father was always picking on me" as one said), or a father or mother who expected more than the child could achieve. If this criticism is not suffered in infancy the effects are not so deep-rooted; nevertheless the results may be serious because the boy may resort to gang activities to find acceptance. An adult with this background tends to be over-sensitive, suspects criticism when it is not intended and reacts indignantly in any case. That is, his ego feels constantly threatened and he has to defend it against attack and undervaluation.

In one such case I had the boy had become an exhibitionist. This had begun in childhood; the urge invariably came after rows with his father who, he said, was always telling him that he would "make a mess of things". The exhibitionism persisted into adult life and resulted in a prison sentence after he had been jilted by his girl-friend. Clearly the act was, in this case, a form of self-assertion, but a regressive form. On the other hand, a child sometimes identifies with the father's or mother's too high expectations and so develops a too strict and tyrannical super-ego.

These are also the effects of over-indulgence to consider, but I have seen very few of such cases in prison, from which I assume that it is not nearly such a common cause of crime and delinquency as lack of love. It can, of course, produce the spiv. He is used to doing exactly as he likes without being answerable to anyone. Consequently he is not prepared to work for a boss but has to be his own master. Often this works out quite satisfactorily, but if not, the young man may go from job to job and finally fall in with work-shy mates and take to easy short cut methods of getting money. The situation will be more serious, though, if the indulgence begins in infancy and the primitive instincts are not disciplined and controlled.

These are some of the effects which can be produced by factors which interfere with normal development and which, therefore, may lead to a-social behaviour. I am, as I hope will have been understood, differentiating them from offences which are simply a reaction to severe prolonged stress and are not due to a personality or character anomaly, and also from the offences or crimes of those whom East called "normal offenders" —those who have a latent disposition for crime, even for murder. The examples I am thinking of are men who, if they could have been helped to sort out their problems at a "reality" level, would certainly not have committed the offences.

NINE

SPECIFIC CRIMINAL MANIFESTATIONS

IN THE LAST chapter I described what may happen when an individual's normal development is interfered with; that is, the anti-social behaviour which may result from certain disturbances in infancy or childhood.

I now want to turn to some of the offences which are due to a specific psychological condition—offences for which there is a well-defined psychopathology. The most common of these are sexual offences, stealing, violence and arson. I am omitting sexual offences as these have already been fully discussed in previous chapters.

Stealing has already been referred to as a compensation for lack of love, as revenge, and a means of attracting attention. There are, of course, simple reactive causes, such as the need to get food or money to survive, and in the case of the "hardened criminal" it is a "way of life". Moreover, thieving is almost inescapable when a boy is taught to steal by one or both of the parents. In such cases, the super-ego functions in an anti-social way because it has introjected the standards of the criminal parents. It becomes what has been called a "criminal super-ego".[58] The psychic organization is like that of the normal individual but because of social factors there is an identification with criminal prototypes.[59] The cases of this kind which I have seen have had a neurotic anxiety for which they were referred for treatment. This was the result of an intra-psychic conflict; for there had been some introjection by the super-ego of normal socialized standards. But the "criminal super-ego" undoubtedly accounts for many "hardened criminals" and recidivists.

Car stealing is a particular form of theft, and it is found mainly among adolescents. Very often it is just a means of having an hour or two's pleasure and excitement, or a car may be "borrowed" in order to carry off goods after a raid on a shop. These offences are generally committed by a few members of a gang. But car stealing by an individual is likely to have a psychological meaning. For the developing adolescent it may represent an assertion of independence, in which the car provides a sense of power. Gibbens considers that this offence is generally committed by over-protected lads from good homes who have to prove their masculinity. He says there are unconscious and in particular, sexual, motivations. According to my experience, the motive in the majority of cases is to reinforce the sense of power, generally in a period of frustration or depression—at least in the kind of lads Gibbens refers to. In other cases a car, and especially a lorry, has been a substitute for a mother—something which provides comfort. Car stealing is then a regression rather than a compensation. I had one such case of an adult where a car had come to represent women in general: here, of course, there was conscious sexual motivation. "You can't trust women but you can trust cars," he said. In another case, a lad had been over-indulged by both parents and he had been his father's constant companion in the father's work with cars in a garage and at home. A police officer had said of the boy that where cars were concerned he was "like a midwife with a child". What he enjoyed about a stolen car was the repairing of it— putting it in perfect order. This was the expression of a feminine trait in him and this showed itself again while he was in prison, in a homosexual relation; his affection for another homosexual lad was characteristically maternal. This homosexual tendency

had not been apparent before but it was nevertheless unconsciously present in his relationship with his father.

Arson is commonly attributed to revenge and as a means of
obtaining sexual stimulation, and revenge is certainly a common
motive. This may be personal, as in setting fire to a hated
enemy's house or car, or it may be revenge against society. But
in my experience, the sexual motive is not so common (though
it was clearly the overt cause in the case of the immature man
described on page 24). Possibly the temporary feeling of power
given by fire raising could be experienced as sexual stimulation.
In one of the not very numerous cases of arson I have treated, it
was associated with depression. This was a man of thirty-one,
the only child of kind and stable parents; his mother, however,
dominated his life and made all his decisions for him. He was
married to an intelligent woman (but seven years older than
himself). They had two children and, according to him, were
very happy. One day he was knocked off his bicycle and suffered
mild concussion. This started headaches which he was still
having when I saw him a year later. This was obviously a
hysterical symptom. He was out of work for six months after the
accident and during that time spent most of the day at his
parents' home. When he got a job he seemed better; but he
began to get interested in the fire-alarm system at the factory
and, according to what his wife told me, he became increasingly
fascinated in seeing the fire engines turn out. Then he lost his
job and became steadily more depressed, restless and difficult
to live with. He told me that on each of the three occasions that
he started fires, he had got "fed up with watching TV" and just
"wandered off". When he saw curtains at an open window, he
set fire to them on an impulse and then rang the fire alarm. The
third time, he was arrested. He said he was beginning to feel
worried about it and would have given himself up to the police.
This man's depression improved with superficial psychotherapy
and mild drugs. Like the other case cited, he was of very
limited intelligence. I believe that sending for the Fire Brigade
and seeing it come at his bidding gave him a sense of power and

compensated for the feeling of impotence and inadequacy he suffered in the regression he had fallen into. The satisfaction that this feeling of power gives has been the cause in other cases of this kind I have seen.

[This chapter was left unfinished. Nothing was set down for the final section on violence, and I believe that something more was to have been added to the two sections above. For the section on violence, the following comments, scattered among Dr. Smart's notes for the book, throw some light on her views. She had not intended to enlarge very much on this subject as extreme cases of violence and sadism were not often referred to her for treatment. She had, however, intended to deal with the case of Arthur (p. 108).]

Anxiety arising from regression due to
1 The frustration causing the regression (with its hatred leading to aggression)
2 The specific anxiety associated with the particular fixation point (paranoid, depressive and others)
3 Presence of dangerous impulses which come up—e.g. cruelty.

Anxiety on genital level leading to regression to oral and anal sadism, that is, aggressive.

Violence
Environmental pattern—home, locality, war, collective pattern. Repressed aggression.
[Victim as] Substitute, e.g. for mother.

Many cases in which specific psychopathology not demonstrable —immaturity and infantile attitude leading to psychopathic. Includes cases of housebreaking, violence, as by-product.

I have had several cases where an offence has been committed as a result of a depressive state. I had one man who had had several convictions for assault or grievous bodily harm. When I talked to him I could hardly get anything out of him—it was as if he couldn't take in what I said or else was refusing to co-operate. Then suddenly the penny dropped and I recognized that this was the retardation of a psychotic depression. In this state he had been extremely irritable and if anyone annoyed him he reacted by hitting out. This man had a course of E.C.T. which produced a most dramatic change in him and he was able to tell me what had been going on. (From a Lecture on *Psychotherapy in Prison.*)

TEN

NEUROSIS OR CRIME?

[Dr. Smart had intended to return to this chapter (as to Chapter 8 and to the chapter on *Success and Failure*) after completing the sections on Treatment. Her belief that delinquent behaviour stems from neurosis is, no doubt, clear by this point in the book: but only the following few notes were actually set down for this chapter along with the several pages of extracts from other works which she had collected under this heading and heavily underlined.]

IN THE FOREGOING sections I have attempted to show how closely delinquent behaviour is related to emotional immaturity. In this respect it is equivalent to neurosis. Delinquency is a symptom of a neurotic state: there is no *qualitative* difference between neurosis and crime.

While among many offenders who do not receive psychological treatment, anxiety is conspicuous for its absence, many who are referred for treatment are acutely anxious. The reasons for this would appear normal and justifiable but it is *what lies behind* these sources of insecurity that has to be investigated. Anxiety can also be inferred when a man requests treatment because he "feels in a mess", is "all mixed up", unable to live as he would like to live, or settle down, or is unable to control his aggression or overcome his feelings of inadequacy. (*Notes for book.*)

[It seems important to note here that Dr. Smart constantly noted *depression*, particularly its incidence during treatment, as a symptom among offenders—as among neurotics generally—in her notes and her reports on prisoner-patients. As can be seen, she often referred to depression in the case histories she describes. She was, I believe, intending to emphasize the significance of its incidence in the section on Treatment as well as in this chapter. Among the works she consulted and from which she copied extracts, may be noted *Depression and Crime* by G. M. Woddis, British Journal of Delinquency, 1957.]

"Psychoneurotic reactions (*psychoneurosis*) are abnormal mental states exhibiting either mental or bodily symptoms and signs, or all of these, which are the result of persistent mental conflict in personal relationships, past or present, in regard to others or oneself and which are susceptible of cure by psychological means, the patient retaining the same view of the real world as the ordinary man; whereas in the types of reaction called *psychotic* the world is viewed in the light of delusional or hallucinary experience, of disorder of thought, or of profound disturbances of feeling." (R. D. Gillespie.)[60]

"When a child's need for love, appreciation and valuation is hopelessly and constantly unsatisfied . . . eventually the situation becomes intolerable. . . . Rather than admit defeat he repudiates the need for love from anybody . . . becomes independent, antisocial, hostile; a hard, self-contained and callous delinquent. This leads to the chronic criminal. There must be no let-up in the reaction-formation or the old basic need for love will emerge and if it does it will produce severe depression[61] . . . Psychoneurosis . . . delinquent behaviour is a symptom. In reaction-formation it is the unsatisfied need that is repressed. In a psychoneurosis it is a *conflict that is repressed*." (J. D. W. Pearce.)[62]

"Because of a social code among middle-class people, which

prohibits the acting-out of one's problems, the middle class person with problems is more likely to be a neurotic than a delinquent." (Howard Jones.) [63]

"The ordinary person is often more potentially criminal than he is willing to believe.

"I have consistently refused to accept the view that the delinquent or criminal is necessarily different from the law-abiding citizen. At the same time I am ready to believe that as our knowledge increases, the conception of the non-sane offender will become more complete." (Sir Norwood East.) [64]

"The anti-social urges met with in the delinquent are normal manifestations of the instinctive life of the small child." (Kate Friedlander.) [65]

"There is . . . no sharp line of cleavage by which delinquency may be marked off from non-delinquency. Between them no deep gulf exists to separate the sinner from the saint, the white sheep from the black. It is all a problem of degree, of a brighter or darker grey." (Cyril Burt.) [66]

"The closer one works with the offender the more one is impressed that crime is not committed as much by choice as by compulsion; that it is not dominated by a rational process but rather inspired and motivated by unconscious pressures." (Ralph Brancale.) [67]

"A majority of children with conduct disorders showed neurotic symptoms, whereas those classified as having neurotic symptoms showed but few and mild conduct disorders." [Neurotic symptoms (given in another quotation from the same source) as: overt anxiety, obsessional and hysterical symptoms, hypochondria, depression; functional disturbances; disturbances of speech; tension habits, gratification habits; outbursts of temper. Conduct disorders: disobedience, fighting, lying, stealing, destructiveness, truancy, sexual misdemeanor and occasional fire-setting.] (W. Warren.) [68]

"There are more neurotics in the groups with better homes."
(W. F. Roper.)[69]

"A delinquent act is founded on the same mechanism that we regularly find in a neurotic sympton." (R. D. Gillespie, quoting Aichorn.)

"We might regard the perversity of many delinquents as an alternative manifestation to a neurosis." (Cyril Burt.)[71]

[It should perhaps again be emphasized that Dr. Smart was not concerned in her work—or primarily in this book—with those whom many people think of as "hardened criminals", those whom she previously describes as "men who have adopted crime as a way of life".]

ELEVEN

INDIVIDUAL PSYCHOTHERAPY: AIM AND APPLICATION

Inasmuch as we are convinced that the individual is the carrier of life, we have served life's purpose if one tree at least succeeds in bearing fruit, though a thousand others remain barren. I therefore consider it the prime task of psychotherapy today to pursue with singleness of purpose the goal of individual development.   C. G. Jung.

PSYCHOTHERAPY HAS BEEN practised in some form or other since time immemorial. It has been the concern of the medicine man and the priest, the faith-healer as well as the quack. It is only in recent decades that it has been practised by doctors and received respectable status as a scientific subject. It is now recognized as a valuable form of treatment both of the neuroses and of psychosomatic disorders. Individual psychotherapy gives special recognition to the needs of the individual in so far as he is different from all other individuals. In this way it differs from counselling and suggestion, which are based on general principles applicable to the majority. These are practised in particular by welfare workers and prison officers who have had some training in group counselling and similar methods, but they are also, of course, part of the armamentarium of the psychotherapist at times.

Individual psychotherapy, however, seeks to elucidate the individual's problems in terms of his own experience and personality.* The aim of the therapist is to help that individual to become more fully himself—as Jung puts it, to bear his own special fruit. Development of the personality, then, may be said to be the ultimate aim of individual psychotherapy.

But in the vast majority of cases, the aim, at first at any rate, is more limited: to relieve symptoms. These may be neurotic symptoms, such as anxiety, depression, phobias, obsessions and so on, or they may be psychosomatic symptoms such as tension, which is converted into duodenal ulcer or eczema or asthma. The relief of symptoms may be expected to result in three things: a better adaptation to reality—to the circumstances of living—greater ability to make satisfactory relationships and sufficient freedom from neurotic conflict to be able to make decisions based on free choice. Lastly, we must remember that the goal we hope to achieve must necessarily lie within the limitations of the patient's own possibilities: we must neither expect too much of a patient nor undervalue his personality by imposing on him our own first impressions of his limitations. The late J. R. Rees summed this up in his interpretation of an ancient Greek saying when he wrote, "to be able sometimes to cure, more often to relieve, and always to make a helpful relationship with patients, is a sufficiently high goal for any of us in the profession of medicine."[73] Nevertheless, this "helpful relationship" may lead to a development of personality that Jung spoke of as the "prime task of psychotherapy today".†

I have already described the conditions in which psychotherapy

* The word "personality" which in general parlance often means no more than an individual's tastes or prejudices, is of course used here in the psychologist's sense of meaning wholeness and completeness of any individual character.

† It is this fact that has impressed me in my work with prisoners. So much more is often achieved by them than would at first seem possible.

is practised in prison, but I would like to emphasize two points. First, that—as in private practice—the patients are seen entirely alone and the strictest confidence is observed (prisoners are often anxious to know that this is the case). Secondly, the treatment is never represented as an excuse for misbehaviour or something to shelter behind. One of its effects may be the release of aggression which may result in a fight, and if punishment is meted out it has to be accepted. In my experience there is rarely any resentment about this, provided the punishment is fair.

My own technique—so far as this term can be applied in psychotherapy—is that of the dialectical method. That is to say, doctor and patient are on a basis of equality: the doctor having no pretensions to superior authority or the desire to influence. He recognizes that the individuality of the sufferer has the same value, the same right to exist, as his own. Together they seek the guidance of the unconscious, which has to be discovered in each individual patient. I emphasize this point because it embodies my own philosophical attitude as well as that of many of my colleagues and it is, I consider, the only kind of relationship which can help another individual to fulfil himself.

I hope after making these points to be able to show how Individual Psychotherapy can produce basic changes in the personality. I would say also that the changes aimed at—and very often achieved—in institutional treatment and group therapy are basically the same as those of individual therapy and some people profit more by the former. If they do, such treatment is, of course, far more economical of time and personnel. But for some, individual treatment is essential and I have seen many men and boys who said they could not adapt to a group or in whom even the best institutional treatment has failed. There will always be the need for individual therapy: what is uncertain is whether there will ever be enough therapists to meet that need!

Psychotherapy is effective at various levels but an immediate and superficial advantage in individual psychotherapy is the patient's appreciation of being able to talk to *someone who listens.* The right kind of listening involves interest, concern and a manifest desire to help, within the framework of a detached and objective attitude. It may be the first time in his life that the patient has been taken seriously and his personality respected— this is especially true of prisoners. It is through this recognition of his personality by the therapist that the patient begins to recognize himself as a person in his own right and this is the beginning of self-respect.

But if this is to be the outcome it is absolutely essential that the development of the personality shall be based on the true self. As we have seen, everybody—from earliest infancy—is subject to certain demands and expectations from their parents and others and these may lead to their assuming a personality which is false to themselves.*

Such cases are seen particularly in private practice because these conditions are likely to produce severe neurosis such as depression and anxiety. I attribute the depression and the guilt which accompanies it (and which gives rise to anxiety) to the suppression or oppression of some vital part of the personality. This is *real* guilt because it comes from the betrayal of the true self—something which can run through every level of the personality. I shall be referring to it again.

Another factor in treatment which I will deal with is the

* This theme is developed by R. D. Laing (*The Divided Self,* London, 1960, p. 104). "The false self is the initial compliance with the other person's intentions or expectations for oneself, or what one feels to be the other person's intentions or expectations. This usually amounts to an excess of being good, never doing anything other than what one is told, never asserting or even betraying any counter-will of one's own . . . a negative conforming to a standard that is the other's standard and not one's own and is prompted by the dread of what *might* happen if one were to be oneself in actuality. . . . The false self may also be absurdly bad . . . a response to what other people say I am." We have seen what bad effects this latter can have in cases where the parents "pick on" the child or always assume that he is "no good".

transference.* It is probably true to say that all psychotherapy (and other forms of therapy too!) is based on the transference in some form. But at first the relationship between patient and doctor is little more than a "*good* rapport". If the rapport that develops is not a good one, therapy is not likely to be effective.

* See Glossary, but also p. 102

TWELVE

PRINCIPLES IN THE PRACTICAL
APPLICATION OF TREATMENT

Reductive analysis

With every patient the therapist must remember that it is the infantile, sick part which needs help: not the more adapted adult part. The patient may be quite unaware of this split in himself.

He may be identified with the sick part or he may minimize it, but it is important that sooner or later he recognizes that there *is* a sick part in him and there have not been suitable conditions for development. For this reason this part of him has remained infantile.

Obtaining a very full and comprehensive history, which will reveal the origin of the symptoms, will take up the first few interviews—and indeed perhaps the bulk of the treatment. This enables a good rapport to be established because the patient becomes aware of the therapist's interest and concern. Later on the history may be amplified or new facts emerge because the patient is unlikely at first to be aware of the significance of the events of his earlier life and may have taken some of them for granted. In the course of the history, the patient's attention is drawn to the circumstances which have led to his present situation.

This approach is a form of *reductive analysis* and leads to an understanding of the origin and development of the symptoms.

At this stage it can be explained that the patient's childish outbreaks of aggression may have been no more than a natural way of asserting himself so as to get the attention he needed. The uncritical attitude on the part of the therapist even to the most a-social behaviour is clearly very important, as it enables the patient to see that this infantile part of his personality must be accepted and not condemned. Above all, the therapist must himself be unshockable, making no judgements at this stage, but seeking to understand what interfered with natural development, the suffering this interference produced and the intensity of the emotions which are still felt with all their infantile strength by the grown-up patient. This may be the first time that the patient has experienced an attitude of love towards the sick part of himself and, as I hope to show later, love is the essential basis for the development of the personality.

It may, of course, be difficult to establish a right attitude in the patient to that immature part of himself. Indeed, the very fact that a man seeks treatment is an indication that he is dissatisfied and therefore intolerant of himself. And it may well be that the idea of improvement is bound up in his mind with the idea of repudiation. The first task of the therapist is therefore to give him the insight and understanding that leads to toleration and acceptance: control and modification of the sick part comes later, and this introduces the concept of reality.

Reductive analysis, therefore, uncovers hitherto unconscious motives and trends. The patient cannot understand *consciously* why he becomes so violently emotional in certain circumstances until these emotions are traced back to their origins. This is a very important part of the effort to reach the goal of greater consciousness—in the psychological sense. The consciousness that has now been gained consists of the infantile desires and conflicts that Freud revealed and which form the basis of psychoanalytic teaching. Dreams, however, provide another very important and direct contact with the unconscious.

Development of the Ego: Deeper effects on the development of the personality, according to the "innate tendency".

What I have been describing is what might be called a creative relationship between patient and therapist. It helps the patient to become aware of himself as a person—that is to say, aware of his ego—and the respect for his personality gives support to the ego. This is what will have been lacking in childhood, possibly as the result of too severe or, as has been pointed out, inconsistent punishment. The emphasis in childhood then has been on suppression—or it may be indulgence—of the demands of the Id (the instincts) rather than on supporting the infant's own ego in controlling these primitive impulses. If that is to be achieved the mother must be strong and firm herself, unafraid of the child's violent emotions, secure in the control of her own: what Winnicott calls "the quiet mother".

So in this work of helping the patient to become aware of himself, the personality and maturity of the therapist are all important. He will have to provide the security that the mother was not able to give and when the therapist has his own impulses well under control the patient acquires the confidence to control his own primitive emotions and gradually becomes able to do so.

It must be remembered, however, that infantile emotions other than pure primitive aggression may be uncovered during therapy. For example if the infant has been rejected or deserted this may give rise to severe depression in later years, together with feelings of unworthiness and guilt. In the course of analysis, the acutely hurt and unhappy infantile part which has been so firmly repressed must be made conscious. Again, these emotions will have the strength and intensity of the infantile experience and may well be overwhelming. The repressed infantile aggression will also come up as an experience of violent anger and resentment. In such cases there is a danger of psychotic depression which means that the ego is overwhelmed by the emotions within. Whether a psychosis* develops or not depends

* See Glossary.

on whether the ego is strong enough to withstand these inner forces. Here again the therapist represents a bulwark that remains unshaken by the patient's violent agitation. He must share in the suffering by understanding the terrible experiences of infancy and he must support and accept the infantile part as he would support his own unhappy child—for then it will eventually feel acknowledged and loved instead of rejected. This function of the therapist belongs very much to the transference. What I have given here is a clinical picture which is more often seen in cases of neurosis than of crime or delinquency in which violent aggression will have been more overt. But, as we have seen, this overt aggression is generally the result of suffering in infancy.

But the ego, because it is the link between the individual and the outside world, does not only face dangers from within. The world outside may also be threatening for it is peopled by adults who make demands—brothers and sisters who feel like rivals for the parents' love and, later, playmates who may be unfriendly and hostile. Quite soon, the infant is brought into touch with outer reality. Development of the "reality sense" requires the need to modify the instinctual demands.

When this has not happened, the reality sense has to be developed in therapy. In prison there are many opportunities for assessing the patient's reactions to outer circumstances. When he can view these situations more objectively—which is to say, more realistically—something important has been achieved.

To the ego, too, belong will and striving. A child's self-will may be suppressed by parents who have an image of their child as obedient and submissive. This may result in repression of natural energy and this may break out later on in a violent form because it has not been modified and brought under conscious control. Self-assertion will be lacking and there will be difficulty in striving towards any goal. The fundamental damage if a child's natural impulses are suppressed (rather than consciously *controlled*) is the violation of its true self, as we have seen. In such cases, self-assertion and aggression have to be given value and supported through therapy—which is not what may be usually associated with the treatment of delinquents. And, of course, the prison environment may well provide the occasion—and the provocation. This may bring on punishment which has a deterrent effect and which further develops the reality sense—in this case the recognition of cause and effect.*

When there is self-awareness, there is the possibility of reflection. The ego is then able to become less the victim of inner emotions and outer pressures. In other words, some detachment is acquired through reflection which makes it possible for the patient to make more objective decisions, based on a truly "free" choice.

[A few days after this sentence was written, Frances Smart became too weak even to dictate, and she died within two weeks. She left headings for the remaining sections of the book, but no synopses to fill them out and comparatively few and unco-ordinated notes for their content. It was not possible to be sure how much she had intended to include from these notes, while on the other hand—as I know from what she had told me— there was much that was to be included for which there were no notes at all.† For instance, we lack nearly all details of the actual processes of treatment, and also of the patients' reactions. Basic theory remains, but much of the evidence supplied by cases (particularly her most recent cases) and on which she set much store, is lost.

Nevertheless, the material which remains is the clue to these final chapters which she herself considered to be the most important of all. To disregard it because it was often frag-mentary would have impoverished what was already written and risked misrepresenting her views.

What I have tried to do, therefore, is to gather together whatever written material of hers I could find that was relevant for the headings she left. This material comes from three

* Cf. the statement by a prisoner quoted by Dr. Smart on p. 95 [Ed.].
† This, of course, was because the material for the remainder of the book was to come directly from her own experience and the conclusions derived from it. It was, therefore, really all "in her own head".

sources: first, the actual writing and the short notes she left for the book; secondly, an article "Reflections on psychotherapy among prisoners" written for *Spectrum Psychologiae*,[74] which was the seed of this book; thirdly, her own lectures and lecture notes. In addition I have included any comments made by her to me in the course of writing the book and a few notes or reports on her prison cases: finally, comments by others who had experience of her methods, and recollections by patients who were still prisoners when I was completing this work.*

Except for the last category and my own linking notes everything which follows here is exactly as she wrote it. Occasionally, therefore, these last sections will make more exacting demands on the reader than the book has made up to this point, since some of the writing included was originally intended for colleagues and students and has not been adapted for the general reader; moreover extracts from other works have not been broken up or simplified. I did not feel justified in making any adaptations without her consent.

Nevertheless I have taken passages out of her articles, lectures and some of the writing intended for the last chapters and inserted them under the appropriate headings rather than reproduce them entirely as they stood. I decided to do this, after much searching of heart, for three reasons: first, because in many cases large parts of the passages intended for the book had already been used in preceding chapters; secondly, because the articles and lectures often duplicated what had been dealt with in an extended form here, and thirdly—and this I feel to be the most important reason—because to reproduce what was left as it stood would have destroyed the shape of the book; the last section would have become simply a collection of statements and the sequence of thought would have been lost. So what I have tried to do is to carry out her known intention, of describing the problem of crime and neurosis and its treatment to the lay reader, by maintaining the original structure—the structure of the book having been conceived for this intention. This

---

* I was able to see these men owing to the kindness of the Prison Medical Authorities. But unfortunately, nearly all Dr. Smart's patients had been discharged or transferred by the time I was able to make contact with the prison.

method of splitting up the available material for the appropriate headings seemed the best way to preserve the book as she had planned it.

(Note: The headings preceding the sections and chapters are those written by Dr. Smart. The source from which the subject matter is taken follows the extracts. Material for the remaining sections of this chapter was particularly fragmentary; greater continuity will be found in later Chapters.)]

The control of the instincts

Expressed in psycho-analytic terms, the offender who cannot or does not recognize the need to control the urge to satisfy his desires when these are in conflict with the needs of society, has not evolved from the pleasure-principle to the reality-principle. As Fairbairn puts it,[75] "The aspect of taking still predominates over that of giving—a characteristic of the early oral phase of development. At this stage the infant's experience of its mother is only of the breast and not of her as a person; that is, it relates to a 'part-object'."

The development of consciousness in man has given him a certain amount of control over his instinctive behaviour. As we have seen* instinct consists of perception of the stimulus object, a specific emotion aroused by the object and a specific behavioural response to emotion. With increasing consciousness, more energy becomes available to the "will" and the specific behaviour response can be modified.

Melanie Klein has shown conclusively that the infant's earliest experience of the breast and of the mother have a profound effect on future development and of relationships in later life. This is the child's first experience of "object-relations". . . . The experience of feeding gives rise to the infant's phantasy of taking in the "good" or "bad" object, which then becomes "internalized"—i.e. is felt to be inside him. This "good" or "bad" object is then, under certain circumstances, projected and once again felt to be a quality of the external object—the mother or

* See Chapter 7.

her breast. . . . The breast is experienced as a "good object" when it satisfies the primitive sensual needs—so long as the mother is at the same time a source of love and support. It is a "bad object" when it is withheld or does not satisfy the infant's needs or if love and affection are lacking. If the "bad object" predominates the child feels overwhelmed and persecuted by badness, reinforced by its own violent hate and aggression. But experience of the outer "good object" strengthens the feeling of a "good object" within . . . these infantile phantasies lay down a typical pattern for that individual of his relation to the external world. (*Notes for book.*)

A prison case: Depression with paranoid content. Very poor slum background. Fear of aggression leading to obsession with thoughts of violence. When people kind to him he resists them. *Rejects the projected bad breast.* (*Notes on prison cases.*)

Many of the younger men . . . are for the first time able to talk to someone who listens and accepts them. I believe the "good mother" is thereby experienced and in the relationship which is established with the "good mother" in the therapist, a basically healthy personality can begin to mature in a normal, non-neurotic way. . . . In many individuals there is a more serious disturbance of the instincts and the offence is an expression of this: for example, in some sexual offences, in the taking and driving away of a car or lorry (when it may represent a temporary regression into the womb) and in some crimes of violence in which infantile destructive urges have broken through. Such cases are often, though not necessarily, due to the effect of an over-protective or a dominating, possessive or cruel mother, and in these cases the father is often weak and ineffectual. This situation is well known to interfere with the development of normal masculine aggression and self-assertion. Again the relation to the "good mother" in the therapist promotes healing of the damaged instinct.

The aggressive instinct can remain unmodified and, what is

more, be strongly activated if a child is deprived of love and especially if it is rejected during the earliest years of its life. As we have seen, aggression is the natural response to deprivation and unless it is modified a petty thief or a dangerous criminal may be let loose on society.

A lad of sixteen whom I have treated for three years, had this background—though he was adopted at three and a half by a couple (they already had one son) whose love and loyalty to him could not have been exceeded by the most loving and enlightened parents. Nevertheless he showed delinquent tendencies from six years old and before this had constantly to be "testing out" their love. He ran away from school and from home, though he always gave himself up to the police and was always glad when his foster-father fetched him. He stole from the teacher's purse and told lies about ill-treatment from his adopted mother. He described the running away as a need to "run away from things". His home, he said, felt like a cage. In prison he was acutely claustrophobic when confined to a cell and he had to be accommodated in a ward in the prison hospital. During treatment he worked out this feeling as far as to say that the urge to get away came from "a searching and a longing for something in a hole inside me". He said he was always looking for something. This, he agreed, was a vacuum where there should have been love and he was for ever hoping to find the love that would fill this infantile vacuum. He was obsessed with the idea of killing and had many dreams of killing and shooting. He wanted to kill whenever he could not get his own way, but in particular he felt he must kill things he loved and, in fact, he killed his own pets. "Everything I like I feel has got to be killed because it might hurt me—I have that much affection for it." This was the only kind of affection he knew and it gives an indication of how deeply he was hurt in early childhood, before his adoption. He often felt suicidal and made one suicide attempt while in prison.

When I first saw this boy, at the age of sixteen, he was serving seven years detention for shooting at a policeman, and he had all

H

the characteristics of the typical psychopath. He was cold and quite "unrelated"; had no concern or care for anyone but himself, no appreciation of the unremitting love of his adopted parents or remorse for his behaviour. If he did not get what he wanted he was not content to wait for it but became intensely angry and, though he was not actively violent in prison, he had been overheard to say that he would find an opportunity to kill an officer and then escape—and it was recognized by the staff that this was not an idle threat.

This boy's aggressive instinct was quite unmodified: it had remained in its infantile and primitive form and it entirely dominated the ego whenever his desires were thwarted. There was practically no development of the super-ego, so there was no check on violent behaviour except the knowledge of the consequences. Fortunately, however, there was the basis of a strong ego which was apparent in his behaviour when the aggression was not activated. In the course of treatment he became independent of other people's opinions and showed a strong will in making a determined effort to achieve a goal. In time this strengthening of the ego proved to be the critical factor in controlling aggression.* (*Notes for book.*)

"If antisocial actions are not punished by the outside world the power of the super-ego is weakened and the danger arises that our own antisocial impulses may break out in action." (Quotation from Kate Friedlander,[76] heavily marked by Dr. Smart.)

Discipline, for example, is the basis for later self-discipline. Self-discipline is not innate. The development of discipline is the product of collective adaptation to reality. . . . If the child is to become socially adapted he has to be taught discipline from outside. It is then introjected and becomes part of his own character structure (just as collective knowledge, like mathematics, or many aspects of modern culture, have to be "learnt"). (*Notes for book.*)

* For subsequent account of this boy see p. 109.

94

Conversation with a prison case. Aged eighteen. Offence—indecent exposure. Suffered from sexual repression.

After being given twenty-eight days in a cell and loss of remission following a fight, he determined to appeal. I agreed that he should take the legitimate way that was open to him to stand up for his own rights for he felt he had been treated unjustly. He said, "That's what I wanted you to say." From this remark the actual event was re-capped and I saw the point of view that the visiting magistrates had taken—that he was "getting revenge" by deliberate planning and not just involved in a fight. Pointed this out to him and he said, "I shall let it go. I won't think any more about it." (From *Notes on Prisoners*: also from a note found among papers.)

Super Ego. At first imposed. Need to correspond to own personality, based on "true self".

In neurosis a feeling of guilt is a very common symptom; with prisoners it is rare and especially in relation to the offence committed . . . When guilt feelings are present in the non-psychopathic offender they generally relate to personal relationships or to some aspect of home life. However, in the course of treatment a sense of guilt often emerges, together with shame for antisocial acts. It is the function of the super-ego to restrict primitive impulses and to limit behaviour to what conforms to the ego-ideal* and is socially acceptable. There is a deficiency of the super-ego in most offenders and this accounts for the absence of guilt feelings. As this deficiency is corrected, the super-ego begins to give rise to conscious feelings of guilt. Many writers attribute the committing of offences leading to conviction to an unconscious feeling of guilt and need for punishment. . . . I consider, rather, that the moral sense of the offender is undeveloped, as it is in a child, and consequently feelings of guilt are absent or inadequate. The super-ego is still unconscious, together with the guilt feelings which it produces. But this is not the result of

* See Chapter 7.

95

regression so much as that it has not become sufficiently conscious and "independent". The ego of the offender is still governed, as Kate Friedlander puts it, by the pleasure principle . . . "The conscience of the delinquent has not yet become independent." (*Notes for book.*)

It is really one's own infantile attitude that holds one captive and when this is relinquished . . . there is a release of psychic energy which becomes available for life—establishing one's own attitude, evaluation and relationships. It is also available for the work of integration of the individual personality, work on the shadow, the animus or anima and so on. . . . (from Talk: *On Being Oneself.*)

I don't think I need to say much about the difficulty we all have in making the shadow conscious and integrating it. But it is in accepting our shadow that we become ourselves. The shadow is the part that is not brought into the light, the shady side of ourselves of which we are a little bit, or very ashamed. Even when the shadow is made conscious, impulses arising from it have to be controlled. . . . The problem then arises for most of us, "How much *should* we be ourselves?" Even when we *can* be. . . . It depends very much on whether the person has to be freed from inhibitions and therefore needs to be encouraged to be himself and react more spontaneously, or whether he is too inconsiderate and needs to learn self-discipline . . . (*Talk*, as above.)

Many men in prison differ in an important respect from the patients met with in general psychotherapeutic practice in that they have experienced and lived the side which is repressed in most people and is properly called the shadow. That is, they have lived the destructive, anti-social, unacceptable, dark side of the personality while the creative and socially adapted part is repressed and remains undeveloped. The problem then is to bring into consciousness and develop the repressed "light" side and enable it to become effective in controlling the unruly, destructive elements. (From Essay in *Spectrum Psychologiae.*)

(A Prison Case) had always lived in a phantasy world as a child. Always had a need to escape from reality, which produced dissociation with amnesia. Had to boast to prove himself. Had dominating mother and was frightened of father. Learnt from her to lie to avoid trouble. (At end of treatment said): "It isn't enough to say I'm not coming to prison again. I am resolved on that anyway, but I want to be happy and to live life. I've begun to face myself. I've never been able to be honest with myself before and I'm not as bad as all that." (*Notes on Prison Cases*. But prisoner's statement quoted from *Talk*, as above.)

[The following comment contributed by a private patient and seems relevant to the section on the emergence of the super-ego.]
"What was so vital in working with FS, vital to her treatment, was . . . the combination of clear moral values with total acceptance and the fullest possible understanding, with being completely uncritical and making no judgements. This does not mean an absence of moral values or standards, but rather allows real ones to emerge in the patient. (This links, perhaps with what she said on the super-ego being based on the *real* self). The fact that "wrong" done is understandable and explicable in terms of a person's life and experience does not remove the wrong. There is no "explaining away"—a perhaps popular misconception of psychology based on Freud's reductive analysis. The reality of absolute values (even if implicit rather than explicitly stated) made a firm framework which gave a most important sense of security: within this framework was understanding and compassion . . . I think it is possible for people to become, in a sense, bewildered by analytical treatment, seeing everything they do and that happens to them as having a "good reason", seeing themselves as quite passive and becoming, in a sense, more irresponsible. There could be no question of this with FS. . . . Her clear affirmation of standards combined with

total acceptance of the individual was very important in her treatment."

Dreams

Patients asked to make a note of their dreams if they remember them. N.B. Most patients get remarkably interested in their dreams and begin to take them seriously and even to interpret them for themselves. It is noticeable that dreams have an effect on changing attitudes, helping self-control, etc.

[Except for the above heading and note, the *Notes for the Book* gives no material for this section, and the prison patients' dreams given here are those described in a lecture and in the essay in *Spectrum Psychologiae*. Most of these are given as examples of *Transference* or of the *Archetypal Basis of Treatment* (see next section and the following chapter). In this section are the few dreams which are specially relevant to her note above. Since there is no material on interpretation, except the occasional comments given with the dreams, I have included the following notes taken from *Notes for Lectures*.]

Dreams are the expression of the unconscious in image form. Not meant to conceal (as Freud says) but to reveal.

Are for the purpose, generally, of modifying, compensating* or changing the conscious attitude. May produce a completely new attitude (as in very impressive dreams).

Interpretation may be on objective or subjective level, according to the context of the patient's life, and the dreams.

Dreams of prison patients. One of my patients, a man in his thirties, had not been out of prison for more than six weeks since he

---

* The dream being an expression of the unconscious, can balance or compensate the conscious attitude to a life situation, taking the opposite side if this is too one-sided or coinciding with it if it is correct or adequate. (Summarized from a long lecture note. An exposition of Jung's method of dream interpretation intended for the "lay" reader can be found in *An Introduction to Jung's Psychology* by Frieda Fordham, London, 1953.) [Ed.]

was eighteen. He was illegitimate and brought up in an orphanage and at fifteen went into the army as a cadet. At seventeen and a half, he went into the adult army because the war was on and from then on he was in constant trouble, mainly larceny and housebreaking. He was discharged from the army because of this and then he committed minor offences in order to get back into prison because he couldn't cope with life. He saw no purpose or sense in anything. He had one good relationship—with a middle-aged woman who, when he was a cadet, invited the boys to her house, and my patient kept in touch with her through the years. She was, of course, a mother figure for him. But this wasn't an intimate relationship and in fact he had had no intimate friends at all and found it very difficult to mix with people. A very important point was reached in his treatment when he spoke about his masturbatory guilt. It was months before he could bring himself to do this and then he felt greatly relieved. Over the years he had had two recurrent dreams. In one he was riding a bicycle and being chased and entered a narrow passage from which he was unable to escape and which became narrower and narrower. In the other he was driving a car or lorry and was unable to change into a higher gear. These dreams quite clearly show his situation. In prison he began to have dreams in which he was cycling along a road but now he was happy and not being chased. He began to make some friends in prison and mix better. When I saw him the day before his release he told me of a dream he had had the night before in which he was on top of a very thick wall which he was taking down, removing it slab by slab. This man got quite a good job when he went out, which was about eight years ago, and about a year ago I heard that he was still in this job, though still rather a solitary individual.

Then there was a lad of twenty who was doing a Borstal sentence for larceny and had asked for treatment because he was a homosexual. His mother was an alcoholic and a compulsive

* Dr. Smart's short notes on prison cases show that a large majority had constantly dreamt of being chased.

thief and from the age of thirteen she had taught the boy to steal and got him to do her stealing for her. Consequently he had had several convictions and had been on probation, in Approved Schools and then had the Borstal sentence, while she had had only one conviction. The father had no say in the matter at all although, apparently, he disapproved. The boy was extremely fond of his mother and when she died, when he was seventeen, he was terribly upset, but then found that he was afraid that he would see her ghost. One night, while he was in prison, he had a vivid dream about her. First she was standing near him and smiling at him, and then she was trying to push her way through a crowd of people to reach him and this woke him up in a panic. This boy responded very well to treatment, and by the time he went out he was beginning to have heterosexual fantasies and was no longer attracted to other homosexuals in the prison. This lad was a rather effeminate type physically and, of course, he remained so but he went out confident and got a job in an office and telephoned to tell me he was getting on all right, though I have never heard if he became wholly heterosexual. As far as I know he has not come back to prison.

A much more serious result of repressed masculine aggression was a case of a young man of twenty-seven, emotionally immature and completely lacking in confidence and self-assertion. [This patient's history and crime is given in Chapter 5, page 33.] The patient came to me about six months after the crime had been committed. He was extremely depressed and could think of nothing but his crime. "*It eats into my mind like cancer*," he said. After about two months he had a dream in which he was swimming in the sea carrying a baby a few months old and desperately trying to reach a boat, as the sea was full of sharks which were attacking him. Discussion about the baby as a new development in himself gave him hope and afterwards he was less depressed. Then there was a dream in which a large black dog (similar to, though bigger than, the old dog he once had at home) came in carrying a small child on its back. The child was crying and the dog walked round the house and then came to the patient, who picked up the child. Then the dog lay down on the ground as if dying. The child in this dream was a girl. Here again his attention was turned towards a new part in himself, this time a feminine part, which could represent the possibility of relatedness to women. Meanwhile the black, outgrown instinctive animal part that was associated with childhood, was ready to die. Finally there was a dream in which a dog and a tiger were fighting. After killing the dog the tiger turned into a large black animal with some white on it and with a ferocious human face. This the patient called "the buffalo-man", half man and half buffalo. It rushed past him and he knew, he said, that it had gone to join the buffalo herd. Later he realized that the human face was his own and he was very disturbed by this. This dream was a turning-point. After he had accepted that the buffalo-man was a part of himself, but was relegated to its own world, he felt and looked better than ever before. He had no more unpleasant dreams, he was able to talk about the crime without excessive emotion and said he was now *"able to live with what had happened"*. In addition, he had, he said, a sense of himself, began mixing well, and said to me, *"I'm satisfied with how I feel now. It's as if I'm coming out of something."* Treatment was terminated soon after this and except for a short period of depression which passed, he continued to be well-adjusted in the prison and reasonably self-assertive. After discharge from prison, he had a very difficult time and went through a bout of severe depression. However, he overcame his difficulties and had medical treatment for the depression and later a letter said he was working hard and, as he put it, getting on with his life. (From Lecture: *Psychotherapy in Prison.*)

Transference

Transference is not the main instrument of the therapy. When the patient is related to his own unconscious he is much less dependent on the therapist (see Hadfield: "Keep the emotions related to the object to which they originally belonged", *Psychology and Mental Health,* p. 420).

[The following definition of transference is given in some of Dr. Smart's lecture notes "In the analysis of the personal unconscious, this consists of projections of the parent images, with accompanying emotional experiences." Among headings for a lecture is described the threefold function for the psychiatrist in the transference: "the projection of infantile relationships": "establishing the human relationship (being accepted)" and the "transcendental function".

[A passage from Gerhard Adler's *Methods of Treatment in Analytical Psychology*[77] is heavily underlined by her: "Generally speaking, transference is not only a mechanism for the re-experience of repressed infantile sexual impulses, but a tool with the help of which the patient can integrate so far unrealized psychic faculties."

In the case of the prison patients it was the first two of the functions she describes above which were most often exercised; but, as will be seen, Dr. Smart was impressed by the number of these patients in whom a deeper layer of the unconscious could be reached. (See following chapter on the *Archetypal Basis of Treatment*.) Her views on transference as a psychiatric technique are stated clearly at the beginning of this chapter. To this may be added the following passage from her essay in *Spectrum Psychologiae*.]

The existence of the transference is of course of vital importance in that it is a relationship through which the unconscious is activated and which gives the patient the security to confront himself. It is a *sine qua non*, where any success is to be achieved, and a "positive" transference* is especially valuable in this kind of therapy. For, after all, the outstanding need for prisoners is to change in such a way as to become more related to their fellow-men and to society and this can only be done by becoming more related to themselves—and this requires relationship to another human being. A man who comes into prison is cut off from his normal relationships and if he is at all concerned about himself, there can be a unique opportunity for

* See Glossary.

forming a relationship with a therapist through which he can find a new relationship to himself and to his fellow-men. As Jung says in *Psychology of the Transference*[78] "relationship to the self is at once relationship to our fellow-man, and no one can be related to the latter until he is related to himself".

[However, another passage from this article—on the healing effect of the unconscious having, in some cases, even greater value than analysis of the transference—is of the greatest importance since it expressed a belief which she held very strongly. From what she said to me I know that she had intended to enlarge on this point in the book. The next chapter on *The Archetypal Basis* will deal more fully with this, but less emphatically than she had intended.]

In many cases therapy follows the conventional course of analysis of the personal unconscious. They are mostly cases of personality disorder in young men and a reductive analysis is called for. Generally the transference is a "positive" one. This is not surprising in the circumstances of a prison environment but I also attribute it to the fact that the negative feelings towards the parents have generally been quite effectively expressed in reality and only need full recognition and understanding. One man of thirty-three who had a long sentence for larceny—his ninth prison sentence for the same offence—had always stolen from members of his family. He recognized that his offences were an expression of his negative feelings towards them and this was fully discussed. He also came to recognize his parents' value and thus accepted them in spite of their shadow. As time went on, he became aware of his growing dependence on me and his desire to please me and had insight into this. On one occasion he said that he felt like a four-year-old child with me and accepted this as a necessary temporary situation. Shortly after he was able to tell his mother, when she came to visit him, that he must break away from her. Fortunately, she accepted this and was even willing to help him—on a conscious level. This man had a dream in which he held a spear in his hand and had to follow it as if it were showing him the way. For several months he kept thinking about the spear and besides recognizing that it represented his emerging masculinity, he said to me one day: "The spear is a strength and straightness which demands and gets respect. At present I see that in you, but I know I have to have it in myself so that you will respect me." A good example of the withdrawal of a projection. (From Essay in *Spectrum Psychologiae*.)

The transference is no substitute for the real thing—the mother's love which should have been given. In the transference, there isn't purely and simply identification with the infantile; there is also an adult consciousness and this recognizes that the transference is not the real thing. So the natural and appropriate resentment against the real mother remains. The transference provides a secure relationship in which these emotions can be rediscovered and experienced and the lost infantile part can develop. (*Note found among papers.*)

[It seems appropriate, at this point, to include four statements made by prisoner-patients whom Dr. Smart was treating up to the time of her resignation from the prison service, as these would have been receiving the line of treatment described so far, but were not—apparently—among those in which the archetype was significantly activated, as in the cases she wrote about in the next chapter.

I have given the first three, which came from interviews I had with these men, as unbroken statements, but I put a few questions, such as "What impression did Dr. Smart make on you?" Did she ask you questions? Did she ask about your dreams? Was there any point where you felt she had shown you something new? Did she give you anything which remains with you and you think will help you in the future?" In each case, however, the men continued talking on their own after the first couple of questions. I saw these men separately and alone. They were all eager to talk about her and give me any help they could: but, as would be expected, their educational or intellectual equipment was not of a kind which would enable them to analyse or closely describe the actual process of treatment, though they they most convincingly testified—to one listening to them—to the results.

All names are fictitious. Dr. Smart's own reports have been summarized.]

Jim (about thirty-eight years old)
[According to Dr. Smart's notes, this man was a typical case of immaturity, due to an over-protected early childhood, lack of confidence and late development of secondary sexual characteristics. (After her resignation, he had surgical treatment which was beneficial.) He had had homosexual affairs though he had more pleasure from heterosexual relations. It was because he wanted to give a present to a girl that he was involved in the crime for which he was in prison, and it was through mixing with homosexuals that he got mixed up in a criminal set. He had also become a chronic alcoholic. Dr. Smart noted that his prison sentence (of several years) would help to stabilize him and that he would benefit from further psychological treatment. Reports after her resignation showed that he had improved psychologically and was steadying down.]

"She was the best doctor I've ever seen. You could talk to her like your mother. You didn't feel ashamed: she knew about everything and wasn't shocked. I began to feel I was getting somewhere about the third time I saw her. She said straightaway, 'Start at the beginning.' I told her how when I was ten my mother died and I went up to her room and saw her and how it frightened me, and then I kept dreaming that I saw her ghost. Dr. Smart made me face my trouble and my fear. You had to come up against the fear and say to it, 'Come out, and what *are* you?'. I kept wanting to have sleeping drugs and drugs to make me quiet but she made me want to try to do without them.

"Other doctors always made you feel they were superior—like

in the army, they must be right and you just answer the questions. And she had a sort of easy-going way as though saying, 'You can talk to me—or you can get out!' I feel *stronger*. I've got something underneath at last. She said to me once, 'Buddhas only point the way, It's up to you to make the play'."

Jerry (twenty-four years old)
[Dr. Smart left no notes or reports on this young man, but she had treated him for about six months up to the time of her resignation from Wormwood Scrubs three months before her death. He must therefore have been one of the men she felt she must help as long as she could. He was serving a sentence for housebreaking and larceny and had been in trouble ever since he was a child. He was treated at six as a maladjusted child and had then been in foster homes having refused to be reconciled to his mother and stepfather. Previous reports, from borstals, had noted that he was aggressive at times and that his larcenies involved people he knew well, following arguments with them: also that there was danger of his becoming a member of the crime fringe unless his insight was broadened. It was noted at the prison hospital, after Dr. Smart's treatment ended, that he felt much more settled. He did not wish to continue psychiatric treatment with any other doctor.]

"What I noticed about her more than about any previous doctor or psychiatrist [he had had psychiatric treatment in a home at one period] was—well, of course she was a woman—but after I'd given her my history she was able to pick up points I'd passed over, which I'd rather suppressed. She had a way of coming in without warning and saying, 'What about *that* occurrence?' perhaps a week or two later. You didn't see her putting it down—she had it all in her head. And it was always something that I found, thinking it over, was important. I remember once how I mentioned a name I didn't think was important and she said, 'I will see you next week. I'm busy now.' I knew she wasn't—we'd only had a short time and she was going to be there all afternoon. But afterwards when I was alone, reading, it suddenly struck me that the person I'd mentioned was important. She never answered a question that she put to you—she left it to you to see and work out.

"I knew I needed help when I came here. I waited a year and then I was put on Dr. Smart's list. My trouble was—I rejected people. Anyone who disagreed with me I just went away from. I wouldn't have anything to do with them. After I'd been with her about three months, I understood that this was my problem.

"She said once, 'There's something you could do to help me. Try and remember your dreams.' I usually don't. But then I did have a dream that I remembered—I think because she suggested I do this. It was about driving down a road and it got narrower and narrower until the car was scraped on each side. She said, 'What do you think this means?' I found I could understand it. Something like that had happened to me, once but now I found I could translate it.

"I used to suppress things when I was in group therapy at the mental hospital and with Dr. Smart I kept things suppressed at first. But she always knew I was giving answers that passed over the real point. She'd say nothing then and later she'd say, 'You said *this* a few weeks ago.' And every time I knew straightaway that she knew what was the really important thing.

"It was a relief to have her know. With most psychiatrists I've seen, they see you for a few minutes and nothing happens. With her I found I'd see what she meant, afterwards, suddenly, when I was alone.

"She didn't only talk about my history. She'd talk about things that happened to her—things like her car, for instance. I knew at the end that she hadn't been well but I didn't realize how ill she was. She never complained of anything or of feeling tired.

"Last Christmas she said she would be away for the holiday and see me after Christmas [this was the Christmas before her death]. I had no contacts outside—but at Christmas there was a letter for me. It was a Christmas card from her. There was no

reason for it and I wondered about it and talked about it when I
saw her again. I said, 'Someone is interested in me.'

"I feel better now than I've ever felt in this situation at any
time. She's made a difference. She gave me a new aspect of
myself. Anyone else I've seen made no *difference*. I always kept
something back with all the other doctors."

Arthur (aged about twenty-nine)
[This patient was a case which Dr. Smart had intended to use as
an example of violence and sadism in Chapter 9. She told me
that she had begun to get a clue to his condition: but she had to
cease treatment, because of her illness and resignation, before
she could get as far as—perhaps—she might have. He was serving a life sentence for the murder of his two infants. He had also
killed pets. He had considerable mental capacity and studied in
prison for examinations. In her notes she wrote that he told her
that he did not know why he did these acts of sadistic violence
and could not recall doing them. He was rational and "intellectual" but had a one-sided development and had no warmth or
relationship with anyone—except his wife. He felt sadistic
towards defenceless creatures—if they had tried to defend themselves, he would have stopped, he told her. The violent acts
"built up" inside him. The treatment (Dr. Smart noted) had
resulted in a slight freeing of his ability to express his feeling and
slightly increased his relatedness, but he was unable to come to
any conclusion on a personal level. Nevertheless towards the
end of her treatment he had a sadistic dream of a "collective"
[i.e. collective unconscious] nature, of torture by a political
party. This suggested to her that the sadism came from a very deep
level which could have produced a psychosis. This was confirmed by the unrelatedness, so the "opening up" was significant.
He had asked for further treatment.]

"She was *nice*. I found I could talk to her—more than to other
doctors, perhaps because she was a woman. I found I could tell
her what I felt and things I had done. She would start me off
with questions and then we had more or less a conversation. I
talked more freely as we went on. All through she asked me

about my dreams. I had a lot of dreams and I hadn't bothered to remember them before, but she told me to try and remember them the moment I woke up and then I found I could. I found the dreams gave me an insight into how I felt about things. She used to try and get me to interpret them—but she probably put some idea into my head when I did this.

"Sometimes I didn't want to see her because I didn't want to talk to anyone then. On these occasions the interview was a flop and very short. Other times we'd go on for an hour or more and when I came out I'd feel *good*—marvellous.

"Psychiatry doesn't mean much to me—there seem to be so many different interpretations. What I trusted was *her* treatment.

"I don't think there was any point where I felt I had understood anything new—though there was something which encouraged me but it wasn't anything to do with her. They gave me a psychological test—one of those things where you look at blobs on a piece of paper. It showed marked improvement. But she didn't seem to take much notice of that.

"When I heard she had died I missed *her* more than the treatment. You felt she minded about you—she was interested in you as a person."

(At this point in our conversation, the prison officer came for him as it was dinner-time. But he came back into the room just after the door had closed to add this last sentence.)

"You know—when my mother came here to see me, Dr. Smart saw her and talked to her. She was interested in *you*."

Jack
[This was the boy whose story is told by Dr. Smart in the section on the control of instincts, p. 93. He again was one of the patients she felt she must see up to the last possible moment. She was deeply concerned about him. She had described his case in her Talk on *Psychotherapy in Prison* a year or so before and had then spoken of him as a psychotic case who was beyond help. By the time she wrote the account for this book, she felt there was more hope (see p. 94). She told me, she intended to use this case as an

example of Treatment: but unfortunately she did not give me any further details and her reports on him are not now available, as he has been transferred to Grendon Underwood. The Chief Hospital Officer, at Wormwood Scrubs, however, gave me the following interesting account.]

"We had thought he was a really hopeless case. But he improved so much with her that we got him to Grendon afterwards—he couldn't have gone there unless there was hope for him. When he came here he was dangerous and cruel. At first he was always trying to get Dr. Smart to recommend him for jobs here which involved his using knives or scissors.

"He got into the way of chatting to me during the last year or two. He always wanted to talk about her. He had implicit faith in her and he looked forward to seeing her. At the end he said, 'It wasn't so much that she showed me the error of my ways, but that what I had done and been *needn't* be so.' He felt he could be a different personality. Before, he'd felt that he never wanted to be different. He came to have faith in himself. That is what *she* did for him."

[The following account was written by Jack. The Medical Superintendent of Grendon Underwood was good enough to tell him about this book and ask him on my behalf whether he would care to write his feelings about and impression of Dr. Smart. He did so without other prompting, on his own, and the account here stands as he wrote it.

From one of Dr. Smart's colleagues at Wormwood Scrubs, I understand that the reports on this boy from Grendon Underwood are promising.] He is due for release on parole by Autumn 1969.

"I was introduced to Dr. Smart by [the doctor], who at that time, was my psychiatrist at Wormwood Scrubs.

"I can't remember what my first impression of Dr. Smart was, as I, at that time, was suffering from deep depression, and was not particularly concerned about what was going on around me. I do remember though that as time went on I began to realize that Dr. Smart only wanted to help me, and was not trying to trick me, as I had once thought.

"What with my temper and the fact that I always seemed to be getting into a great deal of trouble, I must have been quite a problem for her to cope with. But *she never gave up* and I think it was through that very fact alone that I started to gradually make progress. We discussed as far back in my childhood as I could remember, to the present-day happenings. This went on for a long long time. Anything that came up, she would always try her best to help me with it.

"I can't say my change happened overnight. It didn't, it was a long hard process of a number of different things, but my main trouble was coping with difficult situations, without resorting to violence.

"I am very happy to say, I have improved a great deal since then, and I now look forward to living a happy and contented life.

"Thank you, Dr. Smart, thank you very much indeed, I am more than grateful for the help you have given me, for without your patience and understanding I couldn't have hoped to even make a start."

[The following comment on Dr. Smart's "method" of treatment, is contributed by a private patient.]

"There was no ready-made answer to any problem. If one expected a general 'known' answer to one's question, one was disappointed, since, as she said, 'every analysis is different', everyone's case is individual. She joined the patient in a voyage of discovery. She knew the territory which is bewildering to the patient but one's particular path had to be found according to the guidance of the unconscious. She could explain the landmarks and point out signposts; the direction suggested by a dream, the importance of an apparently insignificant picture, the meaning of one's feelings and value of an experience one might otherwise dismiss. Nothing was dismissed. With what she herself spoke of as her 'profound faith in the process' (analytical process) she listened intently not just to the patient but to his unconscious and waited patiently for the development to which it led. She never presumed to 'know' but in this way gave one the knowledge of how to find one's own way. She illuminated it and showed one how to follow it (not least by the example of her own attitude)."

THIRTEEN

THE ARCHETYPAL BASIS
OF TREATMENT

[A considerable amount of material was prepared for this chapter, in which the particularized account of psychotherapy for offenders was to be carried into the wider perspectives of analytical psychology. But this material had not been organized into a complete statement, and there remained a great deal of exposition—and linking material—to be written. What was left for this chapter does, however, extend the outline of Jung's theory of the unconscious, given in Chapter 7, and Dr. Smart had intended to deal with this theory in greater depth in the final chapters of the book. These passages also throw further light on the significance of the dreams and give evidence for her views on transference, particularly that alluded to on page 103 in the previous chapter.]

SINCE THE CONTENTS of the *personal* unconscious are derived from the personal life of the individual they can, theoretically, be made conscious. This is, in fact, the task of reductive analysis aimed, for example, at freeing the young neurotically disturbed individual from his infantile attachment to the parents. The *collective* unconscious, on the other hand, cannot be encompassed by the ego, for its dimensions are infinite and the smaller cannot contain the greater. Its contents, the archetypes, may, from time to time, be experienced by the ego as a wholly irrational and compulsive urge or fear which can be dispelled neither by rational argument nor by reduction to personal, infantile experiences. Then the archetype may manifest itself as an image—an image that may appear to the dreamer (if it occurs in a dream) as nonsensical and even banal, or on the other hand, it may be highly numinous and impressive. (This depends more than anything else on the attitude of the conscious ego.) When an archetype manifests itself, whether as a spontaneous image or in an old-age ritual from time immemorial, as in the spring ceremony of the Wachandi tribe (page 49), Jung speaks of it as a symbol. The archetypes are transpersonal—they cannot be fully known and understood by the intellect or fully comprehended by the ego.

In 1919, Jung spoke of the archetypal or "primordial" image as "Instinct's perception of itself". Later he says that the archetypal image is a representation in consciousness of the *pattern of the instinct* (Collected Works, Vol. 8, p. 201). We may say that "the image represents the meaning of the instinct". (*Notes for book.*)

[The following passage from Gerhard Adler's *Methods of Treatment in Analytical Psychology* is heavily underlined by Dr. Smart.] "To him (Jung) a symbol is not the irreducible fixed translation of a dream element into an image, but expresses a novel and complex fact, which on account of just this novelty and complexity transcends conscious formulation. The symbol acts as a psychological transformer of energy; it is the means by which the mere instinctual flow of energy 'can be utilized for effective work'."

(Comment by private patient)
"You felt that she (Dr. Smart) subordinated her own mind to a greater source of knowledge—to the unconscious. The clues came from this. The reaction you got from the unconscious— whether it helped directly with a problem or not—produced creativity. The attitude of respect and faith you had for it made

you able to live more completely. It was what went on on that level that had authority.'

The cases I have been describing have shown the importance of the personal transference which may or may not need to be interpreted. But I am also very much impressed by cases in which the greatest value is not consciously given to the personal relationship but in which the unconscious is activated and healing is brought about through the effect of the images from the unconscious on the conscious ego. I consider that these are examples of the archetypal or transpersonal transference in which archetypes become activated.

A man of forty-three requested treatment on account of homosexuality. This had started at the age of twelve when he was seduced by an adult male. Although attracted to girls later on, his guilt feelings prevented him from making normal relationships with women. In his thirties he had been "initiated" by married women and found himself to be potent with them. So it was clear before treatment began that he was at least potentially normal. This man came from a good stable working-class home and a united and ordinarily happy family. The patient had done well in the Royal Air Force during the war and after the war in the Royal Navy. After that his activity was speedway riding—a career typical of the *puer aeternus*. He had had a previous prison sentence of four years during which he received treatment at another prison for six months. After that sentence he had further treatment privately for a year. His treatment with me lasted four months and consisted entirely of dream analysis, the first dream occurring immediately after the first interview. Very little interpretation on my part was needed, for rarely have I seen a series of dreams which spoke so clearly to the dreamer. Often the dreams used the symbol of a car, so familiar to him that he readily grasped its meaning for him. Gradually his sexual phantasies became more and more heterosexual and finally he was having no homosexual feelings or phantasies at all. This man had the opportunity of forming a relationship with a woman a little younger than himself who visited the prison regularly and whom he hoped to marry after he was released. This meeting was a synchronistic outer event which was extremely helpful for the inner development. I think this case was an example of the *hieros gamos* which Jung describes in *Psychology of the Transference*.[79] Through the relationship with me, the anima* was activated and freed from identification with the mother. It could then function in its right way, relating the patient to his unconscious so that he was able to integrate the process of emotional development symbolized by his dream images. Freed from the mother, the anima was projected on to a suitable woman to whom he related in an adult way.

One of the most impressive cases I have seen of the autonomous activation of a healing process in the unconscious occurred in a man of forty-eight. He had been convicted of buggery and had had a previous conviction for indecency with a girl, eight years before. He had had a reasonably happy, though tough childhood. He was the oldest of eight, his mother was kind and a good mother, his father was strict and when occasionally he got drunk he was violent. The patient had been married for twenty-three years and had six children—the eldest a married woman of twenty-one expecting her first baby, and the youngest a girl of eleven. The others were boys and had left school. For nine years this man had, as he said, "gone to pieces"—he had been irritable to the point of violence, unable to keep a job, and whenever there was a problem at home he walked out. The boys had been in trouble at school for truancy and later for stealing and housebreaking and had been in Approved Schools and Borstals. His wife, whom I met, was an anxious, harassed woman

---

* Anima and animus are the contra-sexual parts of the personality. The anima carries the feminine of relatedness, tenderness, consideration, caring and patience to wait and allow things to develop. In its negative aspect, it is "moody and bitchy". It isolates a man, behaving like a jealous woman. It is often seen in a man with weak masculinity—it compensates by "throwing his weight about". If a man's anima is still in the mother, he may project the archetypal anima on to a woman and this precludes a human relationship with her. (*Notes for Lectures.*)

and had made a valiant effort to keep the home together. She told me that for a number of years her husband had been unreliable, leaving his job on the spur of the moment; he lost his temper when she tried to reason with him, and he was violent with the boys when they irritated him. Psychiatrically, the patient was suffering from depression, with hopelessness, lethargy, inability to concentrate and very irritable. He described himself as "all mixed-up, yet dead inside", and he was worried because he did not feel bothered by what had happened. At first there was very little rapport between us. Later, he told me: "When I first came I thought there wasn't much wrong with me, but I thought I'd come—it was just another lark. You listened to me and I saw you writing things down and that made me think there must be a pattern. It made me think about myself. Then I talked more than I intended."

I gave him anti-depressive drugs and these, or perhaps the whole situation, had a most dramatic effect. The apathetic depression changed into a very severe agitated depression with intense anxiety and complete insomnia. For a few days he contemplated suicide. Then, in the course of about a month, something happened. Later he told me: "One day at dinner I suddenly saw myself and what I'd done. I left my dinner and went to my cell. I could think of nothing else—I couldn't work properly, I couldn't sleep. I had to think it all out." It was an extremely painful experience and yet he insisted on stopping his sedatives so that he could face his guilt. It was like an awakening. He faced himself and recognized and admitted to himself how he'd failed his family and how the boys' troubles had been due to his lack of guiding them. But he didn't at once come out of the depression. For several weeks he was tired to the point of exhaustion and his mood was very variable. During this time his wife wrote and said she was thinking of getting a separation and then he said he had "given up, couldn't care less, didn't want to know". Then suddenly he saw what he must do. He saw that he had to take responsibility in co-operating with his wife and that whether she left him or not, he must, as he put it, "try and repay". He saw the situation realistically, admitted to his sons where he had let them down and began to exercise his authority with them.

He was very much afraid of meeting his wife lest she be sceptical of the change in him, which he was convinced was deep and genuine. Fortunately, she accepted it and gave him encouragement. There was now an effective contact between his conscious personality and the unifying forces in the unconscious.

During this time his mother had a stroke and became seriously ill. He was given parole to go and visit her in Ireland. His mother died an hour after he reached her and then he took on the full responsibility for the funeral because his father was too old and stricken and his brothers not much use. When he came back to the prison he was depressed and listless. Two days later he woke in the morning and knew the depression had gone and knew he could cope with whatever should come to him. All this took four months and he remained strong and firm in his resolution till his discharge a year later.

With this patient there was no manifestation of transference phenomena nor did the unconscious manifest itself symbolically through dreams or fantasy. But there was a break-through into consciousness of the tension of the opposites and it was his great achievement that he could hold this tension and face the conflict. William James, in his *Varieties of Religious Experience* speaks of sudden conversion (to which my patient's dramatic change might be compared), as "due largely also to the subconscious incubation and maturing of motives deposited by the experience of life. When ripe, the results hatch out, or burst into flower." This patient's irresponsible behaviour did not correspond to his basic personality. He came from a united family and though his father had been a heavy drinker and his childhood had been hard, he had nevertheless had what he called "a good family life" and until the age of eighteen had never been in serious trouble. The regressive behaviour was therefore in direct conflict with his more mature personality which had been repressed and lay in the unconscious, ready "to hatch out or burst into flower". The regression had probably been due to difficulties in his family life which he was unable to face at the time. Jung has said that when there is an unconscious conflict between opposites, energy is withdrawn into the unconscious and an archetype is activated. That is to say, a new content comes into consciousness and the individual is able to take a different attitude to his problems, so that the conflict is resolved by being transcended. In this patient, perhaps the archetype of the man in his role of husband and father was activated. At any rate, a mature and responsible attitude emerged and he recognized and accepted his position of husband and father. In accepting his situation he not only met the demands of outer reality but also his own inner childishness was supported and "fathered".

What has impressed me more than anything else in my work in prison has been the tremendously important role of the autonomous activity of the unconscious to effect healing and transformation of personality. I hope the examples I have given show this. They are by no means exceptional cases.

Naturally, for consciousness to be so deeply affected by the unconscious there must be a suitable attitude on the part of the patient, for example an acceptance of the irrational, humility, and a certain capacity for psychological insight. When these conditions do not exist, therapy must necessarily be on a more superficial conscious level. However, I have been amazed at how often my patients in prison possess these qualities and become interested in their dreams and often try to understand them for themselves. When this is the case, the direct impact of images from the unconscious on the conscious personality has most dramatic and far-reaching effects. This has occurred whether the transference was on a personal or an archetypal level or only, apparently, a "good rapport". In fact, in these cases I have found that the healing effect of the unconscious is of much more value and importance than analysis of the transference, though this may sometimes be necessary. (From Essay in *Spectrum Psychologiae*, and from Lecture, *Psychotherapy in Prison*.)

It may be asked if it is important or necessary to distinguish between the personalistic approach and the archetypal. Does it make any difference in the treatment of patients? For the large majority of younger disturbed people, the need for treatment arises from a failure to establish their own independence—they are still in prison in an infantile dependent relationship to one or both parents. The ego is still under the domination of the human mother or father ... but for young people it is, as a rule, neither necessary nor wise to introduce an archetypal concept. A young person's need is to be helped to get into life. Reductive analysis is invariably necessary for symptoms to be related back to parental influences and the patient's reaction to his parents and repression of his own instinctual needs. The transference situation provides the framework in which the repressed emotions such as aggression and love can be safely experienced and integrated and independence of the ego established. Nevertheless there are exceptional cases, even among young people, when archetypal imagery appears. In such cases I have found that unless a psychosis is inevitable, the developmental process that emerges from this imagery leads towards the development of the ego and adaptation to life. It is as if the process of the emergence of the ego from the self* were taking place in the young adolescent or adult because it had not been achieved in early childhood. It is most important that such archetypal contents should not be under-valued. This would be a serious violation of the personality and could deprive the patient of a highly important and enriching experience of himself. (I had a patient in my private practice who at the age of nineteen, had practically no developed ego. She did not feel herself to be a person and could speak very little about herself. But she painted hundreds of pictures. Gradually out of the background of a cosmic environment with no life existing, a tree and then a horse and then her own self appeared in the pictures. In the course of about ten years she established her own life, married and became a highly creative artist. In this case the development took place entirely by

* See Chapter 15.

"following" the way taken by the unconscious processes—that is to say, "analysis" of the collective contents of the unconscious.) (*Notes for book.*)

[This concludes the section of the book which deals strictly with Treatment and it may be useful here to append a note found among Dr. Smart's papers; a summary which is headed *Approach.*]

1 Causal reductive, necessary:
   (*a*) to show the patient the unconscious history or causes of his illness.
   (*b*) to show him external facts which contribute.
   (*c*) to release psychic energy invested in the neurotic symptom.

2 Prospective or final or constructive—having the goal of the development of the individual.

FOURTEEN

FACTORS MAKING FOR SUCCESS OR
FAILURE IN TREATMENT

[This chapter was never even sketched out. The following extracts from Dr. Smart's article and from a lecture delivered in 1966 give a general view of her conclusions.]

NATURALLY ONE CAN never be sure of success and this has led me to speculate on the reasons for success when it has been achieved. First of all, I have found here as elsewhere that the quality of the human material one is dealing with is of paramount importance (though this quality may not be apparent until the prisoner has left prison and is put to the test.)

The criminals who are quite correctly labelled "psychopaths" . . . can be models of good behaviour when circumstances are favourable, but immediately fall into a childish and irresponsible form of behaviour when faced with difficulties. They have no sense of personal failure or guilt and psychotherapy, with our present knowledge, has little or no lasting effect. In another category are those who show real concern and co-operate extremely well and show exceptional insight—intellectually at any rate—yet when they go out they very soon fall back into the old pattern, much to their distress and disappointment.

With some of these I have come to the conclusion that the patient's behaviour during treatment was an unconscious acting out of the "good little boy who tried to please mother", which would naturally hinder any true individual development. In other cases, treatment has not reached a deep enough level and the emotions have not been activated. Others, however, need further treatment after discharge—either continuation of deep therapy or at least some support. It is by no means easy to arrange this and often the prisoner does not wish to receive treatment elsewhere. Whatever his quality, it is asking a lot of a man, however genuine has been the process of inner development and gaining of insight, to go back into the environment which activated the behaviour that brought him into prison and there maintain a different standard.

Every effort is made by social and welfare workers to ensure that the environment on release shall be as helpful as possible: *but a great deal more needs to be done about this*. All the more remarkable, then, when a man goes out of prison, fends for himself, overcomes temptations and, above all, comes through the difficulties of finding a job and lodgings—neither of which is easy for an ex-prisoner—and does not succumb to the easy way out (From Essay in *Spectrum Psychologiae*.)

The protectiveness afforded by institutional life . . . makes it difficult for a man to take up the responsibilities of life when he goes out. This is not such a problem with open prisons, of course; the Home Office have made some provision for this in recent years by instituting a hostel scheme. At several prisons there is a hostel where selected prisoners serving a sentence of over fourteen years can live for six to nine months before discharge while working in ordinary jobs outside the prison. They go out each morning and they can also be out in the evenings and they can go home at week-ends if they live near enough. If they want, they can carry on the job after they have left prison and in the meantime they can find digs if necessary and get used to work outside. In addition to this prisoners have a week's home leave within a few months of discharge which gives them an opportunity to look for a job and make contact at home. . . . But, considering the difficulty of adjustment, which is even worse for neurotic individuals . . . I am amazed at how well they do cope.

In several cases where I have had the opportunity to see a patient if he has come back to prison again, I have seen a marked change for the better, as if the previous treatment had initiated a process of maturing which had continued. Further treatment has then been most rewarding. These have been cases where there has been a neurotic condition of some kind either directly expressed in antisocial acts or contributing to this behaviour. It is impossible to say what is the proportion of such cases in the prison population, but certainly those that receive treatment form a very small proportion indeed. (From Lecture: *Psychotherapy in Prison*.)

[We can find circumstantial evidence of some points made in this general statement in a few of Dr. Smart's notes and reports on prison cases and in the comments made on examples given. In Chapters 12 and 13, for instance, are cases of men whose basic quality emerged under treatment and who were thus able to overcome their psychological difficulties. A singular example, of a case who appeared even to Dr. Smart to be almost psychopathic and yet who was (apparently) saved by the emergence of a "strong ego", is that of "Jack".

On the other hand, I found several notes on prison cases (which were too scanty to be usefully transcribed for this book) in which she had commented "unsuitable for treatment" or "prognosis very dubious" and this was usually because the man was suffering from so deep a psychosis that it was impossible to make a relationship with him and he totally lacked capacity for insight. In other cases, again, treatment could not be sustained for long enough to achieve activation of the emotions or any confrontation with reality. This was often due to the shortness of sentence or to transfer to another prison (sometimes owing to the prisoner's own wish to be nearer his home.) It is worth noting that she treated "Jack" for several years.

There are two or three notes left under the heading of "Recommendations," most of which are purely sociological, such as "Increased facilities for youth activities: education, housing", etc., without any comment added. One, however, runs "Facilities for after-care and continuation of treatment by the same therapist". Many of her reports showed that very often indeed she emphasized the need for continued treatment after the prisoner's release and that many of the men were anxious to continue it. But in fact, as she herself regretfully admitted, this really vital measure in the prevention of crime cannot be put into operation with our present inadequate resources for rehabilitation. Even those men who felt urgently the need for continued treatment (and the sense of urgency could easily be lost among the pressures and anxieties met with on release) often could not find a doctor who would treat them—or the right doctor—in new surroundings; and they often did not remain in the neighbourhood of the doctor who had treated them in prison (even if there had been available funds for such intensive treatment as individual psychotherapy). I do not think, from what Dr. Smart has told me, that any prisoner returned to her for treatment after release, though a few kept in touch with her (one of them gave her a John Piper reproduction which she treasured). But, in her mind, this recommendation was a matter of vital importance—as indeed it is for any doctor who undertakes psychological work among prisoners.

"Success" and "failure" are risky words for the outsider to use in the context of psychotherapy and I would wish to be very wary of using them or drawing conclusions about Dr. Smart's cases when she had not herself pronounced on them. One difficulty here is that she gave no names (except, occasionally, fictitious ones) when instancing cases, so that it is impossible to trace records of ex-patients—in any case the records of released men are almost impossible to get at. As she says earlier in the book, it is never quite safe to make ultimate judgements since there is so little follow-up work possible and unless there is a reconviction it is rarely possible to know anything about a man after he leaves prison. It will have been noted that she wrote that in several cases "if a patient has come back to prison again have seen a marked change for the better". To the layman this may appear, at first sight anyway, a paradoxical statement: but —as may be perceived from this book—to a doctor who knows the degree of conflict from which his patient is suffering and, in particular, the distinction between the various causes of crime —need, depression, aggression; social or psychological—a reconviction does not necessarily mean a loss of what was gained before: though in one or two cases she noted that what appeared to have been gained was not deeply enough rooted—a case, sometimes, of what, as we have seen, she called "good little boy who tried to please mother".

Again, as can be seen from examples given in the book, there were many cases where, in the course of treatment, buried conflicts, aggressions and depressions were activated and at that point again it might appear to the layman (though not necessarily to the doctor), that treatment had not been "successful". But if treatment were allowed to go further and a deeper level reached (as, again, in the case of "Jack" and, I suspected, "Jerry") there could be a remarkable change. A case where such a change did not, apparently, take place seems to be that of "Martin"(p. 61) where the aggression was observed by Dr. Smart in prison but totally and tragically emerged after his release. Since she did not live to complete the account of "Martin" in this chapter, one can only speculate on whether the date of release cut short the treatment before the degree of the psychosis became clear—or else before the man was brought to a condition to control it—or whether our lack of resources for follow-up and after-care deprived him of protection from his own aggression and, most tragically, his victim.

One aspect of rehabilitation (which might well consolidate "success" in treatment) which engaged her mind was that of the re-establishment of the prisoner with his family (cf. the account given of the case on p. 117f. She was deeply concerned that the patient, on release, should be able to re-enter his home with confidence, taking up his responsibilities fully and receiving affection and trust as a father and a husband. This concern, and others connected with rehabilitation, led to her correspondence with Dr. Harry Wilmer, Clinical Professor of Psychiatry at the University of California School of Medicine, and Consultant to the California Department of Correction and San Quentin Prison. Dr. Wilmer had carried out experiments in group psychiatry at San Quentin. Dr. Smart had guarded views on the long-term effects of group psychiatry except for certain types of individuals (though she admitted that with the small number of doctors available, individual treatment for all prisoners was impracticable at present). But Dr. Wilmer's experiment in group treatment of prisoners and their families was a different matter and it seemed to her to be a most valuable pilot scheme for working out means for re-establishing the family life of a prisoner and his life in the community. She had, not long before her death, obtained Dr. Wilmer's permission to include the following summary of an article he sent her, in this book. This chapter now seems an appropriate place for it.[80]]

During the first year of the project, thirteen inmates, their wives and thirty-five children aged two to seventeen years, met monthly at the prison. A staff of two counsellors, a correctional officer, a psychiatric nurse and a psychiatric consultant led the groups. "We were concerned about the children's probably distorted awareness of their fathers' status as convicted felons. Since half of these parents had not told their children that the father was a prisoner, we believed the children suffered from separation anxiety, compounded by deception. In helping the mothers to help the children face the reality . . . we acted on the premise that deception and living a lie foster a sense of guilt . . . that such a deception might be at the root of tendencies towards delinquent behaviour. . . . There is evidence that simple imitation of the father is less important in producing criminality than is rejection by the father. . . . Prisoners, fearing rejection [by their children] counter by rejecting the child first. It was also found that the mothers' attitudes to the children were affected (e.g. some used the child's affection to assuage her own deprivation).

"We hoped to provide a healthy social encounter for parents and children and to give the children the opportunity to re-establish peer relationships with other children to whom they need not fear revealing their fathers' status. . . . We believed that if family relationships could be re-established while the father was still in prison, the inmate could re-enter family life after release and make the transition back to community life more successfully."

The families met one Saturday a month for two hours. The total family met first for thirty to forty minutes. This was followed by meetings of three separate small groups—husbands and wives, children over nine and children under nine. This again was followed by a visiting period during which all families met together with the correctional officer present. The parents' group was modelled along group psychotherapy lines: the small children's group was informal—usually the children played games. The older children's group was a discussion group. The total family group was informal discussion.

The families reacted with enthusiasm: only a few remained sceptical or felt threatened. The young children took delight in the groups, dressed gaily and urged us to have them more often. They formed attachments with the staff. Within four months, parents were urging new members who had not told their children about the fathers to do so, giving testimony to the relief their own families had felt after telling.

The programme proved immensely useful to the staff in evaluating the inmates and the family stability and in making more rational recommendations to the parole board. The meetings also had a good effect on the weekly husband-wife meetings. These groups were able to discuss formerly "taboo" subjects. One inmate said, "I have never been able to talk to my family but now it seems as though in this large family group we can finally talk about things which have bothered us all this time."

"We also saw this group strengthen family ties which could . . . enable the paroled father to think and act as a responsible, rather than an isolated, family member." Nevertheless, there were critical times during the project. Also changes in staff caused serious handicaps. But the results did show the great value and potential benefit of the programme (which had to be ended because of the total turnover of the treatment staff). "Because of the complexity of family groups in prison treatment programmes, we believe it imperative that such programmes be undertaken only by experienced group therapists with the consultation of a participating psychiatrist. In settings in which such programmes cannot be established, visits by the entire family should be encouraged and facilitated. . . . Family group treatment in the prison should, ideally, be supplemented by group treatment of the entire family after the prisoner is released on parole."

FIFTEEN

WHAT LIES BEHIND THE TREATMENT

[The final chapter in the scheme for this book was vaguely entitled "Philosophy", but Dr. Smart usually alluded to it as "the chapter on What Lies Behind It" so I have retained this less formal heading for the fragments which remain for it. The chapter was, for her, to be the key to the book: the ultimate explanation of symptoms, treatment and results. The beliefs she was stating were not simply the fruit of very intensive study, in psychology and psychiatry and philosophy and in many parallel fields, nor solely a reflection of her acceptance of Jung's philosophy. They were also the fruit of her own experience: of the experience of the human beings with whom she had come in contact.

At the risk of editorial intrusion, I feel it is necessary to say this because to some readers this chapter may not appear to be clinically sequential to the preceding part of the book and it might be asked why it should have been included, particularly since it is incomplete. There are, I believe, two reasons for doing so.

The first is that she was earnestly determined that this subject-matter should be included. Some of it, even, was originally drafted for Chapter 7 and then put aside for a final chapter. (A part of this has already been placed in Chapter 13, "The Archetypal Basis of Treatment", where it seemed more immediately relevant.) The very last words she dictated referred to "my notes on Neumann's ideas, particularly of Uroboros" and "How Maternal temens (Uroboros) are restored in analysis"—and in which notebook these were to be found.

Secondly, I believe that what is contained in this chapter will enlarge understanding of what has already been written here: for instance, her emphasis on the "activation of the self" through the unconscious as seen in the chapter on the Archetypal Basis of Treatment, and the emphasis on infantile deprivation and the importance of the mother in considering the cause and treatment of neurosis and crime. If she had lived to complete the book and fill out the many passages which have had to be merely indicated from brief notes, there would have been more discussion of other and more immediate causes for imbalance and impaired personalities. It is noteworthy, for instance, that she heavily underlined this passage from Gerhard Adler's essay on *Methods of Treatment in Analytical Psychology* (previously referred to): "Every such conflict can, of course, be regarded as having its cause in the past, but there are many specific situations where it proves much more fruitful to try and understand and interpret the pathogenic conflict as expressing the present." Nevertheless, beyond and behind these causes, lay her conviction that where there existed a potentially "normal" personality, it was this failure in maternal warmth, guidance and discipline—that is, love—which caused distortion or weakness.

In this belief she was not alone, of course. But she was also immensely concerned to link this with the clues to human development which are found in mythology—the archetypal images and the correspondences found in the myths and in primitive religions and rites—and again to show connection between all this and the stages of development which led to the attainment of what Jung called Individuation, or wholeness of personality. For although Frances Smart was a highly competent doctor, a supremely practical counsellor, who never gave the abstract answer to the concrete need, or spoke in transcendental terms when practical terms were required, her eye was always on this wholeness and the need to find it as the final goal—for herself and for others: though it was not often, of course, that she even had the opportunity of indicating the path towards it—and rarely in her prison cases.

In this chapter are transcribed all the notes—some of them fairly extended—which concern the "transcendental" and mythological origins of her beliefs about treatment. They are, of course, incomplete and too many links are missing. But if read as a continuation of Chapter 6 and 7 and the chapter on the Archetypal Basis, they will be found to extend the ideas suggested there.

The notes here are transcribed as she wrote them and the diction is often more technical and the theories more summarily presented than she would have intended to leave them for publication. Also as I personally know, she intended to break up and comment on the quotations given here, absorbing them more easily into the text and giving them a fuller context. But, as I have already said, I do not feel justified in changing anything she left written, although, in this chapter, where a few passages have been omitted because used in other parts of the book, I have inserted joining phrases. These are in square brackets.]

In 1931 Jung had already recognized the importance of the collective unconscious in child psychology. "The child's psyche," he wrote, "prior to the stage of ego-consciousness, is very far from being empty and devoid of content." The original basic contents of the personality are those of the collective unconscious and he attributes the remarkably meaningful mythological dreams of three- to four-year-old children to "the last vestiges of a dwindling collective psyche".[81] It is out of this "ground-work" of the collective unconscious that ego consciousness develops: "The unconscious is the matrix out of which consciousness grows." Later, Jung speaks of this unconscious substrate as the Self: "The Self, like the unconscious, is an *a priori* existent out of which the ego develops. It is, so to speak, an unconscious prefiguration of the ego."[82]

This concept has been further developed in recent years, particularly by G. Adler, Fordham and Neumann. Adler compares the development and differentiation of the ego from the matrix of the unconscious as the individuation process undertaken in later life. Fordham [as shown in Chapter 7] sees the self as the original archetype in infancy and says that as consciousness develops "the Self sinks more and more into the background and it appears as if the Ego takes its place".[83] This occurs through a process which he calls "deintegration". (Not disintegration, for the self cannot disintegrate—"only the ego can be destroyed or split in pieces"). Deintegration is a spontaneous division of the self: "A desire of the self to become conscious, to form an ego by dividing itself up." These separate parts are, he says, at least related to the archetypes and form the first fragments of the ego.

The total personality (as we have seen) consists of Consciousness, the Personal unconscious and the Collective unconscious. It is the centre of this that Jung called the Self. But, he says, "the Self is not only the centre but also the whole circumference which embraces both conscious and unconscious; it is the centre of this totality, just as the ego is the centre of the conscious mind".[84] The Self therefore has a *transpersonal quality* and can only be experienced symbolically. It represents *wholeness and completeness,* where opposites are no longer separated but united to form a whole.

The image of the Self often appears in dreams as an abstract figure such as a circle, a sphere, a quarternity or a mandala, all of which express wholeness. It may also be personified as a numinous or ideal figure such as Christ or a child—a human or divine figure which is whole, that is, "perfect". The child, as a Divine Child or Christ archetype, still has its original wholeness being yet undifferentiated,* while the God-man symbolizes the highly differentiated personality who has achieved wholeness through suffering. He embodies the opposites which have come together in him—human and divine, spirit and instinct, mind and matter. . . . Fordham also refers to the child's choice of "scribbles", especially a mandala, from which comes a sun-like figure and then a human being. This is not drawn from

* See Glossary.

perception of a human being but arises from "inner libidinal development".

I consider that the infantile fantasies of which Melanie Klein* writes which, as I understand, are assumed [by her] to be of the outer object of the breast [i.e. "personalized" fantasies] correspond in fact to Jung's archetypal images [i.e. transpersonal]. Certainly in some individuals the image may be of a much more symbolic character. This was the case with one patient whom I treated, whose paintings and active imagination took her back to a traumatic feeding experience when she was a month old. The imagery in this case was mainly abstract and there were certain shapes, such as a diamond-shaped quadrilateral inside an oval, which "felt" like her centre—the place where she was whole and secure. This corresponds to the idea that the earliest archetype to be experienced is the Self. Nevertheless, the image of the Self may well be in the form of the breast, with its centring on the nipple—a simple mandala in fact.

Neumann[85] attaches great importance to the early relationship between the ego and the self. He says, "The cardinal discovery of transpersonal psychology is that the collective psyche, the deepest layer of the unconscious, is the living ground-current from which is derived everything to do with a particularized ego possessing consciousness: upon this it is based, by this it is nourished and without this it cannot exist." Corresponding to Fordham's "deintegration", Neumann speaks of "fragmentation of archetypes" and he says of the collective unconscious that it is ". . . as though the inconceivable multiplicity of its aspects had been divided up into the separate figures of the collective unconscious, in order to become experienceable for the ego, either successively or in the aggregate" . . . "The split-off archetypes and symbols," he says. "are now easier to grasp and assimilate, so that they no longer overpower ego-consciousness." The fragmentation of an archetype is, in fact, a distinguishing of its "bewildering variety of contradictory aspects. . . . A developed consciousness can recognize these qualities, but

* See pp. 48 and 92.

originally the archetype acted upon the ego en masse, in all the undifferentiated profusion of its paradoxical nature."

I now want to show that there is an archetypal basis for the need of secure containment in the mother. In his book, Neumann has drawn a parallel between the development of consciousness in the history of mankind and in the individual. He shows that in each case the same archetypal factors determine the course of this development. "The psychic development, or misdevelopment, of each individual is governed by the same primordial images which determine man's collective history. . . . The *beginning* can be laid hold of in two 'places:' it can be conceived in the life of mankind as the earliest dawn of human history, and in the life of the individual as the earliest dawn of childhood."[86]

The original state of complete unconsciousness before there is any differentiation of opposites—light from dark, earth from heaven, male from female—is represented in creation myths throughout the world. A universal image is that of the circle formed by the snake which eats up its own tail—The Uroboros. This is the perfect round, the womb, "where the psyche has her pre-worldly abode, the time before the birth of the ego, the time of unconscious envelopment, of swimming in the ocean of the unborn". This is the "ocean of the unconscious" out of which the infantile ego "emerges like an island for occasional moments only, and then sinks back again. So early man experiences the world". "The ego feels fully contained in this primordial symbol."[85]

Compare this with Winnicott's "circle of love and strength"[87] in which the baby needs to live at the very start. Containment and protection in this "ocean of the unconscious" is necessary on a personal level for everything newborn, whether a seed or a human embryo. For the newly developing human being it is a vital condition both of the pre-natal and post-natal state. In this secure, protective and nourishing environment of the Great and Good Mother, ego-consciousness can begin to evolve and the ego begins to differentiate itself from its environment. This is the nourishing and protecting aspect of the Great Mother.

At a slightly later stage, when the ego is beginning to be differentiated, Neumann says that the Uroboros also represents the World Parents. Hitherto, according to creation symbolism in many parts of the world, "the World Parents, heaven and earth, lie one on top of the other, spacelessly and timelessly united, for as yet nothing has come between them to create duality out of the original unity. The container of the masculine and feminine opposites is the great hermaphrodite, the primal creative element, the Hindu purusha "who combines the poles in himself".[86] "The World Father is joined to the World Mother in uroboric union and they are not to be divided." Then there is a movement "the procreative thrust", and ancient texts speak of the breath of life, self-fecundation of the god. This is the creative impulse, the new beginning. Thus the uroboric Great Mother takes on a phallic, fertilizing quality. "Breast and lactic flow are generally elements which can also appear in phallic form, because the milk is then understood symbolically as a fertilizing agent."[88]

This movement is also the beginning of the separation of the World Parents: the differentiation of opposites—male from female, earth from heaven—which is the beginning of creation. "In all peoples and in all religions creation appears as the creation of light."[86] Light represents consciousness, a state of knowing and being, both for mankind and the world and for the individual. For the individual, then, the fertilizing procreative quality of the uroboric Great Mother at this stage gives birth to ego consciousness.

This is the archetypal basis on which normal development of the personality begins to take place.

This pattern may, however, be distorted when actual personal experiences in infancy do not correspond to the conditions necessary for normal development. This brings me to the last theoretical point concerning maternal love that I want to speak about. It concerns the activation of the archetypal image. It has already been referred to in connection with the instincts,* in which it has been shown that an outer object in experience is necessary for the release mechanism to activate an instinctive "pattern of behaviour".

Every archetype has two opposing aspects which, from the point of view of the ego, are the positive, creative and the negative, destructive. This is true even of the archetype of the self. For example, the collective unconscious, represented by the self-image may overwhelm a weak ego, resulting in a psychosis. The Great Mother archetype, no less has its negative aspect when, for example, in certain circumstances it imprisons the embryonic ego and hinders its natural development. So, when the ego is still under the domination of the human mother or father it corresponds to a failure to free itself from the uroboric Great Mother. [This situation is alluded to at the end of Chapter 13.]

I hope these theoretical considerations will throw further light on *why* "good mothering" in early infancy is so profoundly important. But this is no easy achievement for a young mother. She must herself be able to handle her own emotional difficulties, personal complexes—perhaps dating from her own infancy and childhood. Her relationship to her husband must be reasonably satisfactory and certainly her social conditions such that she can give sufficient time and attention to being a good mother. As Winnicott says, "The [good] mother does not involve her baby in all her personal experiences and feelings. Sometimes her baby yells and yells until she feels like murder, yet she lifts the baby up with just the same care, without revenge—or not very much. She avoids making the baby the victim of her own impulsiveness. . . . Over and over again, a mother deals with her own moods, anxieties and excitements in her own private life, reserving for her baby what belongs to the baby."[89]

This demands a great deal of emotional stability and maturity in a young mother and if this is rare, it is nevertheless a

* See Chapter 6.

goal at least as important for the mental health of future generations as social reform!

These, then, are the ways in which the human good mother
reflects to some extent the uroboric aspect of the Archetypal
Great Mother: she nourishes and protects, she safely holds the
infant in the roundness of her embrace and she contains his
aggression, thus helping him to handle his own frustration and
primitive instincts.

[But ultimately], the chief importance of recognizing the
archetypal, collective unconscious is in the development of the
personality in later life—the development which Jung has called
the individuation process. While development of the ego and the
freeing of it from the complexes of the personal unconscious—so
that a satisfactory adaptation to life can be made—is the highest
achievement for the majority of people, there are some who feel
dissatisfied even with this. In his work with adult patients Jung
noticed that even when the therapy was terminated the analytical process (or what he called "the dialectical discussion with
the unconscious") still continued with some and when he met
such patients after several years, he was impressed at the
development that had taken place. Or, in some cases, the
patients wanted to continue their analysis with him as an
exploration of the unconscious, in spite of being clinically free of
symptoms. He was thus led to the conclusion that "there is in the
psyche a process that seeks its own goal independently of
external factors".[90] Experience showed him that this goal was
the wholeness of the personality, represented by the image of the
self—that hidden and as yet unmanifest "whole man".[91] "It
might equally well be called the 'God within us'" he says in
another place,[92] and goes on, "The beginnings of our whole
psychic life seem to be inextricably rooted on this point, and all
our highest and ultimate purposes seem to be striving towards it."

For these people in whom Jung saw a further development of
personality taking place there had been recognition and relation to the archetype and the collective unconscious.

Neumann says in this connection, "It is necessary for the structure of personality that contents originally taking the form of transpersonal deities should finally come to be experienced as contents of the human psyche. . . . If, on the other hand, transpersonal contents are reduced to the data of a purely personalistic psychology, the result is not only an appalling impoverishment of individual life—that might remain merely a private concern —but also a congestion of the collective unconscious which has disastrous consequences for humanity at large."[93] Here Neumann presumably is referring to the collective upheavals of mankind, such as wars and race hatred. (*Notes for book.*)

Nevertheless . . . the individual whose vocation it is to develop his personality must be faithful to his own inner law, in so far as that is the highest and best that he knows. Social adjustment demands a full participation in life. Jung once said to me, "The purpose of life is to live." Certainly his psychology gives no support to those who would evade the responsibilities of life. (From Speech: *A Tribute to Jung.*)

SIXTEEN

ON BEING ONESELF *

[Two drafts fully written out were made for this lecture. One was shorter (presumably to fit into the time) and I have knit the two together. I have also omitted some details of the cases she uses as examples to preserve anonymity.]

THE SUBJECT OF this talk came to me some months ago when within one week two patients expressed themselves in the words "I can't be myself". Put in one way or another, this is, of course, a common complaint and I felt I wanted to think out the things that made it difficult to be oneself. This paper therefore contains nothing new, but merely some of my observations and conclusions put together.

Being, or not being, oneself may be seen by others or only felt by oneself—not necessarily both. One may be made to feel one is not being oneself by someone else: that may be (I think) part *of* being oneself. On the other hand, there is the person whose defences against being themselves, i.e. of letting others know them, are only too obvious and often irritating. But if the individual is also defending himself against self-knowledge, then this uncomfortable sense of not being himself may not even be conscious. But this is another story.

* A lecture given to the Analytical Psychology Club, London.

My thoughts for this talk fall under three headings. First, freeing the ego from childhood influences. Second, freeing the personality from the tyranny of one's inner figures—differentiation of the ego from the non-ego and widening consciousness—and third, reorientation.

The two patients I have referred to illustrate the binding and paralysing effects of parental influence. Mrs. A's parents expected perfection from her when she was a child and never showed any appreciation. If she did well in a lesson, her father said, "Why weren't you first?" Later, her stepmother undervalued and blamed her.

The other patient M was the eldest son of an aristocratic family. His mother was entirely conventional and out of touch with her own reality. She was never affectionate, nor loved him for himself, and she showed approval only when he behaved as a conventional eldest son.

In both these cases a pattern was imposed from very early childhood.

A child's need for love and approval forces it into the kind of behaviour pattern that he hopes will win love and approval. Or, if this is beyond his capacities and he rebels, he at least gains attention by bringing down anger and disapproval on his head. In either case, the child's own personality is not recognized or given any value and the child himself, hoping for love and security, denies the expression of his own natural spontaneous instincts and urges and replaces them by behaviour which is false to himself.

In some people, this state of affairs persists and the outer shell becomes more and more rigid and inflexible. Such people will go through life, if they are lucky (or unlucky), meeting every situation in a conventional way. Anything which threatens to break through their increasingly thicker barrier, is met with horror and dismissed with perfunctory generalizations. They remain untouched.

If, however, the barrier is not quite thick enough or the individual inside rebels a little, one gets various symptoms such as headaches (or, as in two very good examples that I have seen, a skin rash). Such patients may be sent to a psychiatrist for treatment because the condition is presumed, by a process of elimination, to be psychogenic, but it is often impossible to penetrate below the surface and reach the poor little starved neglected personality underneath. Often it is better (and, in fact, often the only thing to do) to let such a patient keep his symptom, because a revelation of himself and a confrontation with the real state of affairs might be disastrous. Such an opening up, in fact, may be achieved only by some quite shattering catastrophic event. Good luck to the person who is not forced to go into himself! And indeed Jung says that analysis should never be entered into unless there is an urgent need.

Otherwise these people must be allowed to live their conventional lives, turning a deaf ear to the starved and neglected child within. But such people are pathetic: irritating as they are, they need our sympathy and understanding, for it is perhaps the best they can do.

However, fortunately there are many people who seek and desperately want help not only for their symptoms but for a crying need from within. The two patients I have quoted are examples. Now the difficult work begins. Because it promises the only security the person has ever known—the security of parental attention—it seems to him an impossibly dangerous thing to let go, in the slightest degree, of that pattern of behaviour that seemed to be the only way of ensuring love and approval. Moreover, all one's associates carry the projections of one's critical and exacting parents and it is desperately important not to displease them. All efforts are directed towards gaining their approval: but the greater the effort the less one is accepted and given recognition by one's fellows and the more one feels an outcast, hopelessly inferior and isolated. And indeed such a person *is* hopelessly inferior to real people. A conventional pattern of behaviour is no substitute for the real thing.

In the first example, the woman, there was a preoccupation with obsessional thoughts of guilt. She believed she had no value and was always in the wrong. In the second example, the young man, the result of the pattern was lack of any confidence among his contemporaries, paralysing self-consciousness and a feeling of inferiority. Behind these symptoms, of course, there was the unconscious identification with the superior role that was imposed upon him—that of being the eldest son—and the fear all the time of not living up to this, and being rejected. The fear in such a case is the infantile fear of losing the mother's love. To the young child this represents complete disintegration and death and that is why the fear is so devastating and paralysing.

Now I consider that a feeling of inferiority is to be taken seriously, as a challenge. Somewhere, one *is* inferior. This young man was actually of quite superior intelligence, with great gifts: he was, in actual fact, in no way *inferior* in quality to his fellows. But the feeling of inferiority meant that he was not being all he could be and should be. He felt inferior because he was a *feeling type*, working among intellectuals who were predominantly *thinking types*. On their ground, he *was* inferior. The thinking function is more often the superior function in men. But to relinquish his efforts to emulate his fellows was like casting himself upon the waters. Even to make a single truly spontaneous remark required an enormous effort and screwing up of his courage. But when he did so, his feeling of achievement was equally out of all proportion. If he had given due value to his feelings, his intelligence, sensitivity and artistic gifts, he would, in fact, have been superior to many of his contemporaries. This he knew with his mind.

Now to make a spontaneous remark is to give voice to one's real self and for the person who can never be himself, this is a great achievement. But, in such a person, the superior function still lies in the shadow and lacks differentiation. Consequently, it is difficult to have confidence in it, and because it has been suppressed for so long it is even difficult to know about it or to experience it. Such an individual has not begun to know himself and this is the first task he has to undertake. Then he can begin to have the courage to *be* himself—here and there if not all the time.

The feeling of being inferior can be seen constructively and teleologically and not simply relieved by reducing it to childhood experience, though certainly this must be done as fully and completely as possible. But the feeling indicates also that there is an area which should be further developed. One can make capital out of the distressing symptom by looking into oneself and trying to find this area. It is a call to find out what one really is, to [advance to] further consciousness and towards individuation.

This lack of confidence is sometimes precipitated when two people of opposite types are together. One sees this quite a lot, in marriages and among friends, and it is particularly paralysing for the partner with the weaker personality. I have seen married couples where the difficulties come between, say, the husband who is of the sensation type and a less mature person than the wife who is of the intuitive type. Such a husband may constantly criticize his wife's lack of order and her difficulty in dealing with details of everyday life—since she is a *feeling* type with strong intuition and insight. The wife may be very fond of him and try very hard to live up to his standard of practical efficiency. This, by nature, she will always find difficult, so she loses confidence in herself, feels inferior to him and feels she is not being truly herself—when she would not feel inferior. What is lacking is appreciation of her valuable qualities of feeling and intuition. These aspects of her personality are taken for granted by both her husband and herself and only her weaknesses are noticed by both.

Freeing the personality from the influences and patterns of early childhood is a universal task, at any rate in a Western culture. That is why reductive analysis is very important and is generally undertaken first. Indeed these influences can never be wholly eradicated and they will keep cropping up. But at least recognition enables us to handle them.

I now come to my second heading: the analysis of the shadow, and the animus or anima; that is, freeing ourselves from the tyranny of our inner figures, differentiating* the ego from the non-ego and widening the consciousness. For, when we are possessed or dominated by one part of the personality to the exclusion of the rest, we feel "not ourselves", not what we want to be and know we could and should be. When this state of possession takes the form of a mood or of losing our tempers we say "I wasn't myself".

A situation which makes one unable to be oneself and which probably most of us have experienced, is when we receive someone else's projections. Perhaps the commonest example of this is in relationships between men and women when the animus or anima is projected.† This is, of course, a very positive thing as a rule and a means whereby a very important part of the personality is activated. But sometimes the projection doesn't fit and this gives rise to a feeling of being inadequate or falling short of what is expected of one. The individual will try, if the situation is not recognized, to live up to something that feels untrue with resulting discomfort, loss of confidence and anxiety. But here again, I believe that there is a challenge. For if the projection is so wide of the mark that it is absurd, there is no emotional response at all. I think that if negative emotions are aroused, it means that the person should look into himself and see if there is not an inner need for further development in that area. As Jung wrote (*Two Essays*), "The sense of moral inferiority always indicates that the missing element is something which, one feels, should not be missing, or which could be made conscious if only one took enough trouble. Whenever a sense of moral inferiority appears, it shows that there is not only the demand to assimilate an unconscious component, but also the possibility of assimilating it."[94]

I had a woman patient at one time, in her early middle age, who had a very severe incapacitating obsessional neurosis dating from quite early childhood. From that time she had felt terribly

* See Glossary.
† See Glossary.

inferior to other people because, she thought, she wasn't any good at any practical thing: it was not only herself, moreover, but her family also who made her feel deeply ashamed because they didn't manage the practical side of life at all well. The factors entering into the case were manifold and I am only using one aspect of the case to illustrate this point. At school she loved Arts subjects and was not so good at Science and Maths, but she had a friend she much admired who was practical and sensible, excellent at Maths and a good horsewoman. My patient felt determined to show that she too could be good at practical subjects, so she went over to the Science side and in fact managed to get a degree in a science subject. After she graduated she became more and more incapacitated by her illness and was unable to take a job which involved responsibility. As her history showed, by her competitiveness as well as her symptoms, she was completely dominated by the animus, but she was so identified with it that she could not see this.

Then she had a dream. It was in three parts and in the first part she was listening to the radio. A ceremony was being described in which a boy of fourteen was being presented with a silver model of a horse. Then she was watching television and a boy of about seven was riding a horse, dressed up in clothes of another period. Finally, she was actually at a horse-show and the winner was an army man riding a horse that he was quite unable to control.

I am not going to analyse this dream in detail but just give you the patient's own analysis of it, because in this case that was the all-important thing; for the dream brought home to her, without any word from me, the dominance of the animus.

The symbol of the horse immediately made her associate the dream with her friend. Her spontaneous interpretation of the dream was as follows: in the first part, in which she heard something over the radio—that is, more remotely—her friend is represented as a silver model. (I would say the friend's libido is represented thus.) Then everything comes a little closer—it is seen over TV—and here there is the boy "dressed up" and not quite himself. (I would say here, controlling the libido.) Finally the dream reflects reality—the horse-show itself—where the instincts, under the domination of the animus, are quite out of control.

The patient herself recognized from this dream that she was being lived by her animus and the dream showed her how she had surrendered to the animus years before when she took up a competitive attitude in relation to her friend: "I'll show everyone that I can do it too."

This patient had done a great deal of active imaginative work in painting and modelling and later in writing, and later in her treatment she expressed herself in a painting in which she depicted a circle. At the centre of the circle she felt she was in close contact with herself, as for instance, when she was writing her fantasies. But when the outer world made demands on her she had to come to the periphery of the circle and there she felt battered and could no longer be herself. For example, as a way of adapting to her family she had, since childhood, been accustomed to adopting the role of hearty, cheerful extroversion because her family and friends called her a mouse. She even tried to deceive herself by putting on this mask when she was depressed or frightened of something.

This patient had such an urgent need to find her real personality that she was being forced by her illness to keep as much as she possibly could within the circle. . . .

This brings me to the theme of our attitude to the shadow— the rejection and disowning of the shadow, which is really, I think, the basis of this whole subject.

I don't think I need to say much about the difficulty we all have in making the shadow conscious and integrating it. But it is in accepting our shadow that we become more and more ourselves. The shadow is the part that is not brought into the light, the shady part of ourselves, of which we are a little bit, or very, ashamed.

The shadow will always cause us disquiet until we accept it

and give it a place in our lives. I like Dr. Barker's way* of looking at the childish, neglected or shameful parts of ourselves. He speaks of these parts as members of the inner family, and they behave like children and have to be parented like children. They are most important and precious and they need to be cared for and loved as well as disciplined and controlled. Without them we are not truly ourselves. Even when we become conscious of these aspects of ourselves, we are generally ashamed of them, afraid that they will not be approved of or accepted by society. In other words, we care more for what other people think of us than we do for our own selves. When we love the praise and approval of other people more than we love our own inner family, we are betraying ourselves. But just as becoming a real parent demands greater maturity, so the work of recognizing, accepting and integrating our inner children demands a mature attitude, a relinquishing of our own dependence, without which we cannot give support and security to our inner family. That is, we cannot bear to confront the shadow.

The feeling of uneasiness, of "not being oneself" is sometimes the red light which signals the need to attend to the shadow and give attention to something within which is crying out to live. If we reject and disown such a part, we are betraying our own real nature. "To thine own self be true," says Shakespeare's Polonius, "and it must follow as the night the day, thou canst not then be false to any man."

The persistence of parental influence I would compare to bindweed or ivy growing on an apple tree. It retards growth and makes the fruit small and stunted. But even an apple without these disadvantages must always be an apple and never a pear or damson. (Jung said that animals are the most moral creatures because they are true to themselves) ...

There are people who are consistently and uncompromisingly themselves, having supreme confidence that what they are, by nature, must be good. They are non-introspective and never

* The late Dr. Culver Barker, a distinguished London Jungian analyst [Ed.].

spend time reflecting. Provided such an individual conforms fairly well to the collective norm, they are generally very popular and it is certainly easier to cast off restraint and inhibitions with such a person. Sometimes they commit terrible social blunders and for the most part they are quite unaware of it, and generally society is tolerant and they get away with it.

Someone I know is such a person and for myself I find her most refreshing. One feels her to be real, in good relation to her instincts, and wherever she goes people respond to her spontaneous realness and become more themselves. But she makes enemies and is often severely criticized. And, in fact, there is much to criticize because much of the shadow side is so patent and obvious. She is almost entirely without insight because she rarely reflects. Consequently she is not aware of the effect she has on other people. She has, fortunately, a good social persona which, however, she wears lightly and casts off all too readily and when her impulses rise to the surface in a place that touches her closely, like criticism of her family, social requirements are cast to the winds and she is then indeed an *enfant terrible*! But above all, she is utterly true to herself and would no more betray or let down her inner family than she would her real human family. She loves and accepts herself and she therefore has a large capacity for loving and accepting others.

In other people, a high degree of integration is achieved by a natural wisdom used in reflection and self-imposed discipline and adaptation. Perhaps these are the introverts and the others the extroverts. Esther Harding[95] describes such people in these words, speaking of the bearing and dignity of an integrated person:

> The really great among mankind have it, and sometimes quite simple persons, who have no claims either to special goodness or special worth, yet are so completely what they are that the simple dignity of their state of being carries the weight of psychological maturity and an impress of worth beyond any effect of good works.

The problem then arises for most of us, How much *should* we be ourselves even when we *can* be? We all have impulses which are destructive and which have to be held in check. It is indeed a knife-edge on which we walk; a problem which each of us as an individual has to try continually to solve—the reconciliation of the conflict between one's own personal need to live what one feels oneself to be and the demands of society, of the milieu in which we live.

One can't generalize about this. The conflict lies within the individual and no one outside can judge. It depends very much on whether the person has to be freed from inhibitions and therefore needs to be encouraged to be himself and react more spontaneously, or whether he is too inconsiderate and needs to learn self-discipline. But I think that the all-important thing is that we should be as *conscious* as possible of what we do. Sometimes it is possible to make a conscious decision, in full awareness of the needs of our own personality. The spontaneous reaction cannot, of course, be a conscious decision. But it can be reflected on later, in full consciousness. Spontaneity *is* being oneself though it may be only part of oneself. *But it is by our spontaneous reactions that we come to know what we really are.* We know ourselves by being ourselves.

Also, our spontaneous reactions are important for other people. One of the ways in which we have an opportunity to know ourselves is through other people's reaction to *us*. Let us not, then, be too anxious to deprive other people of our reactions to *them*.

The criterion seems to me to be one's loyalty to one's own inner family. It may be a betrayal not to show anger or, on the other hand, the angry child within may need to be helped to conform.

At our last meeting, Fr. Anthony Bloom told us that the men who were referred to as "fools for Christ's sake" were deliberately provocative. Sometimes when we *have* to obey our inner law to be ourselves, we are unconsciously provocative, causing people to reflect and become more aware of themselves.

We also owe it to the people in our immediate environment to become conscious of the shadow and not keep it repressed. I remember Jung once saying: "I determined that I would not make my son live my shadow." He was referring to the really terrible effects of repressing the shadow when it should be made conscious. He gave me an example of this, which I think is mentioned in one of the Seminars. He was talking about this to someone who said he had a friend who was a clergyman who didn't seem to have any shadow side at all. He knew him well and had never seen anything unpleasant about him. Jung was puzzled. Then he asked about the man's wife, for he knew that it might have affected her and caused her to become neurotic. But no, she was quite a normal and well-balanced person. Then Jung inquired about the family. The elder son was very successful—but the younger son was a criminal. Jung says that if we don't take responsibility for our shadow it has to go somewhere, and then we may force someone else into living it.

I haven't up till now used the term persona though one might say that any mask which hides "real" personality, whether voluntarily or involuntarily, is a persona mask.* I would limit the term persona to a mask which represents a collective role that is required by society—or a collective consciousness. The development of a persona is a necessary adaptation and it has to be used in a collective situation. Even so, it can well express the personality, like a coat which conforms to the general fashion, but nevertheless is somewhat individual.

But if the persona is too rigid and is not readily discarded when it's not needed, then the personality underneath does not have a chance to develop along its own individual lines. A persona may be used as a substitute for individuality, and as such it is very seductive. It is seductive because one becomes identified with it and believes oneself to be all the mask represents. Unfortunately society often fails to recognize this state of affairs and pays tribute to such a person, who therefore becomes more and more inflated.

* See Glossary.

Nevertheless, we are all human and we can only see ourselves a bit at a time. The personality mustn't be over-weighted with shadow. That is why it is so important for the ego, built as it is on the conscious adapted part of the psyche, including the superior function, to be strong before it can face the non-ego.

We all of us need some barrier at times to protect us from the horrible reality of our real selves.

Lastly, I want to make it quite clear that by "being oneself" I do not mean individualism. I'll give you a few examples of what I mean by that.

Lady Diana Cooper in her Memoirs describes the activities of the gay and lively group in which she moved in the days preceding the First World War. She says: "Our pride was to be unafraid of words, unshocked by drink and unashamed of decadence and gambling—Unlike-Other-People, I'm afraid."

Professor Joad has written a book called *The Pleasure of Being Oneself*. Here he describes incidents and habitual activities which have given him special pleasure throughout his life. Some are simple pleasures of childhood, though even these are rarely innocent but derived from some peculiarly annoying mischief. Others are derived from getting the better of other people by fair means or foul—mostly foul, but many of them are pleasure-able just by virtue of being different from other people's and especially shocking to ordinary conventional human beings. His pleasure, he says, is in not conforming to what Society would have him be or, as Lady Diana Cooper puts it, in being "Unlike-Other-People".

This need to be different, to emphasize a particular individual characteristic is a feature of immaturity, for it is a way for the ego to acquire importance and to save itself from being submerged by Society's demand for normality. Jung says: "Individualism means deliberately stressing or giving prominence to some supposed peculiarity, rather than to collective considerations and obligations."

Where does all this get us? Those of us who are analysts have to give our patients the help they need, as far as we can. In any case, all of us here go as far as we can in our search for our real selves. We who are analysts are particularly likely to get caught up in the phenomena of our patients' analysis. But let us never lose sight of the essence of what Jung's psychology stands for—of the individuation process.

We do not need to go very far along the way in order to realize that it is a "way of life", but the further we go the more we know that it is true, because it is our own way. Jung has written, "The way is only the way if you find it and follow it yourself."

The individuation process leads to the centre of the individual personality, and it leads to totality.

I now come to my last heading, Reorientation. I call it this because here the centre of gravity of the personality changes. It is no longer the ego that reigns supreme and is all-important, but the Self. Always, the standpoint of the ego must be maintained, but the standpoint of the unconscious must also be appreciated. It is now no longer a matter of an analytical process but a *way of life* which Jung calls Individuation.

The three categories I am talking about are not stages of analysis, nor chronological steps but, rather, different levels on which the freeing of a personality can take place. Sometimes all levels are reached at the same time: through dreams which can be interpretated: through transference which can supply a relationship in which a patient is freed from childhood influences, or from an animus or anima problem—all of which means that he or she is freed for living: but again, this means a way of life for the patient. I recall a case of a prisoner patient who had had more than one sentence and had lived all his life in an unreal fantasy. He said, "It isn't enough to say I'm not coming to prison again. I am resolved on that anyway. But I want to be happy and to live life. I've begun to face myself. I've never been able to be honest with myself before and I'm not as bad as all that."

Individuation means that we should be more and not less able to adapt to the milieu in which we live. This is because the qualities of the personality which become developed and differentiated are themselves collective qualities but it is in differentiating them that we become really ourselves and realize our uniqueness and our original potential wholeness. "A plant which is to be brought to the fullest possible unfolding of its particular character," said Jung, "must first of all be able to grow in the soil in which it is planted." And as he said to me once "The purpose of life is to live".

Experience of a new centre of the personality has the quality which Rudolf Otto calls *numinous*: of the same stuff as religious experience. It is not for nothing that Jung finds parallels to the individuation process in the great religious systems of the world. But only a small number of people recognize it or experience it in this way. Many come into analysis because of an urge towards this as a way of life and religion may have failed to satisfy this urge.

In this part of the work the analyst carries the role of the transcendent function, bringing the conscious and unconscious together. As Otto said, the experience of the numinous can't be given to anyone: one can only help them to come nearer to being able to experience it themselves.

This reorientation results from the voluntary self-sacrifice of the ego, and we know by many parallels that the death of the hero results in a renewal, or re-birth.

It is more than a sacrifice of the instincts, as is symbolized in the Mithraic ritual of the slaying of the bull. The instincts, for modern man, have in any case to be sacrificed to the collective mores. The sacrifice of the ego is symbolized by the death of Christ, the whole, natural man, with his consciousness and possibility of free choice.

More simply: we surrender to the laws of our own nature. That is why individuation brings us close to our own unique reality.

There results a transformation of the personality. A new sense of proportion, a new outlook. Transformation of the natural impulses comes when this reorientation takes place.

It is on this level that the opposites are brought together. Body and spirit, individual and collective, conscious and unconscious, are no longer in opposition, for the middle way which does justice to each is to be found when the individual is oriented to his supra-personal centre, the self. To help individuals towards this is a vocation—and our highest contribution.

APPENDIX

FRANCES SMART was not strikingly impressive in appearance; almost she gave, at first sight, an impression of anonymity. She was a smallish figure, neat, brown-haired, round-faced and with a touch of Midland in her light voice. But this anonymity was dispelled at the very moment of greeting by a quite unusually beautiful smile which established as immediate a sense of communication with the stranger as with the patient or the friend. It seemed to be, and I believe was, a smile of pure pleasure. She was sure and quiet in her movements and she could sit and listen in complete repose. She never showed a hint of restlessness or strain—or even fatigue, until the last weeks of her life. Another quality which contradicted her appearance and also her basic shyness and her almost exasperating modesty, was the gaiety which broke out irrepressibly at times in a happy—an almost childlike—giggle.

She had a complete, absorbing concern in whoever was talking to her, a peculiar intentness in her listening, and for patients there was no barrier, no professional detachment in her manner to them. But also there was no softness: she had great compassion but none of the condescension that can be sometimes implied by pity. And this direct, unpitying concern carried with it a most reassuring common sense. She was very much aware of the concrete, day to day difficulties which bedevilled the resolves to gain emotional or mental stability and she had little time for abstractions which bypassed the practical and material or the generalizations which classified instead of examining. I once gave her an account of a lecture I had heard by a very eminent psychologist who had talked in terms, it seemed to me, of unbelievably jejune classifications. "Oh *X* . . ." she said with exasperated amusement, "he's full of theory and he hasn't *one ounce* of common sense!'

It was, I believe, this common-sense, on-the-spot, element in her which gave her such quickness of understanding: she could pick up a clue, immediately: she could, for instance, in discussing this book—even a couple of weeks before her death when she was very weak—catch the intention of any comment or query one made, however inadequately expressed, and make a clear, unfussed decision upon it. Her power of concentration enabled her to grasp a process or understand an idiom of speech or thought which was strange to her. (Except, I remember her saying once, "I feel such a fool if I am being driven by anyone and have to map-read—I am utterly *stupid* at it and it makes them so cross with me.")

She had little knowledge of—and no marked interest in—any of the arts except where they related to her philosophy. But this did not, strangely enough, produce aridity in communication with her, perhaps because she was direct and non-diffident about her ignorance and always had a curiosity about what was new to her. Also her own range of knowledge and experience had such depth of texture and she had such capacity for gaiety and for ordinary human exchange that, for me at least, every re-union, even the scantiest lunch-hour dates, were lively and warm. Indeed it is hard to understand how she ever found enough time in her fifty-eight years to cover so much ground. When she took up psychiatric work she spent more than half her time with private patients as well as working in the clinic and in hospitals, and later she added the prison work. Eventually she limited the number of private patients but she was still working at full pitch. She worked in the evenings at home, and a good part of every week-end, and took modest holidays—though after her first operation some ten years or so before her death, she took a longed-for voyage round the world. But to go to the country for a day, sit in a garden or take a bus-ride through Sussex villages gave her such delight and such refreshment that one realized how little time she normally gave herself for rest.

This book meant a very great deal to her. She felt that what she had learnt and had done (and I think her work at the prison was a potent element here) had now come to have a definable and definitive meaning for her: that new knowledge and experience was summed up inside her and was her own. The book was an expression of her sense of vocation and its completion mattered more than anything else. She was only a little way through when it became clear that finishing it was to be a race between her physical strength and the cancer. Yet when every ounce of strength had to be preserved she continued to attend the prison. I pleaded with her to resign—"There are some men I *must* help as long as I can," she said. And to another friend she said, "I am worried about a boy. I must do all I can." And when she was finally too weak to leave her bed, she wrote out her reports for the prison authorities. Whatever she did, she did effectively and completely at all times.

I have stressed this effectiveness and this down-to-earth common-sense quality because, as readers of this book will have seen, there was a strong transcendental element in her which underlay her treatment and her beliefs. She was a convinced adherent of Jung's transcendental philosophy as she was of his system in psychological practice. To those she could treat on this level, turning to the authority of the unconscious, she gave renewed life and vision: to those who needed counsel she gave wisdom and the fruit of her medical experience, drawing, when it was needed, on the help or the discoveries of the pathologist, chemist and physician.

Her years at Zürich were a new and marvellous experience. She had grown up and been educated in a provincial town and had practised as a doctor in Birmingham. She was a very reserved provincial young woman. In Zürich she learnt to relax and take in the social pleasures and the strange and exciting new scenes—the old buildings, the mountains and lakes. Above all, she was in close contact with Jung and with his fine and scholarly wife. She used to describe, sometimes, the happiness of their home. There is no need to say how deeply she revered them and the depth of her personal affection towards them. Her friendship with her analyst and teacher, Professor C. A. Meier, was a lasting support.

Perhaps the most telling impression of the impact that this quiet, rather shy and unimposing individual could make comes from the prison officers who saw and talked to her two or three times a week for many years when she crossed the bleak court-yards of the prison to the little cubicle in the shed-like building where she saw her patients or when she came over to work in her room in the hospital wing.

"Oh yes—we all remember her here. We liked her. She was a very *good* woman."

"She was very *good*—everyone liked her. But she could be very tough with the men, too. Some of these chaps gave her a terrible time—always at her for drugs, never let her alone. She must have been tired out very often. But she never gave way."

"She was a really marvellous person. We thought a lot of her here—we all liked her. The men all liked her. Of course, there were some she couldn't do anything with, but there were cases we thought quite hopeless that she helped a lot. And sometimes she had a very bad time with the worst of them, at first. They'd swear at her terribly and once or twice she was actually physically assaulted, but she'd be back again next week just the same to see them. She was never frightened."

Not very long before her death, perhaps with an underlying fear that she would not live to complete the book, I said to her lightly, "Just how would you sum up the treatment?" and she replied, almost lightly too and smiling a little, "It's just love."

B. C. B.

NOTES

1. Carr-Saunders, A. M., Mannheim, H., and Rhodes, E. C., *Young Offenders*, Cambridge, 1942, p. 7.
2. Healy, W., *The Individual Delinquent*, Chicago, 1915.
3. Aichorn, A., *Wayward Youth*, London, 1951.
4. Burt, C., *The Young Delinquent*, Cambridge, 1943², p. 4.
5. *Ibid.*, p. 188.
6. Bovet, L., *Juvenile Deinquency*, U.N. Health Org. Monograph Series, 1951, p. 145.
7. Rees, J. R., "Mental Variations and Criminal Behaviour", Radzinowicz and Turner, eds., *Mental Abnormality and Crime*, Cambridge, 1944.
8. McCord, W. and J., with Zola, I. K., *Origins of Crime*, New York, 1959.
9. Glueck, S. and E., *Unravelling Juvenile Delinquency*, Harvard, 1950, and *Family Environment and Delinquency*, London, 1962.
10. McCord, *op. cit.*, p. 80.
11. Morris, T., *The Criminal Area: a Study in Social Ecology*, London, 1957, p. 172.
12 Pearce, J. D. W. *(op. cit.)*, *Mental Abnormality and Crime*.
13. Burt, *op. cit.*, p. 209.
14. Eysenck, H. J., *Crime and Personality*, London, 1967, p. 39.
15. East, N., *Society and the Criminal*, London, 1949, p. 88.
16. Pearce, *op. cit.*, and other contributors, passim.
17. Warren, W., "Conduct disorders in children", *British Journal of Delinquency*, 1950/1, p. 167.
18. Henderson, D. K., in *Mental Abnormality and Crime* (*op. cit.*).
19. Williams, D., "The Electrocephalogram in the Evaluation and Diagnosis of Criminal Psychopaths", *Prison Medical Journal*, London, Dec. 1966.
20. Court Brown, D., "Sex Chromosomes and the Law", *The Lancet*, 1962, p. 508.

21. Casey, M. D., *et al.*, "Y.Y. Chromosomes and Anti-social Behaviour", *The Lancet*, 1966, p. 860.
22. Forssman, H., and Hambert, X., "Incidence of Klinefelter's Syndrome among Mental Patients", *The Lancet*, 1963, p. 1327.
23. Roper, W. F., "A comparative study of the Wakefield Prison population", *British Journal of Delinquency*, 1950/1, p. 18.
24. Friedlander, K., *Psychoanalytical Approach to Juvenile Delinquency*, London, 1947, p. 27.
25. Storr, A., *The Integrity of the Personality*, London, 1960, p. 46.
26. Wickes, F., *The Inner World of Childhood*, London, 1930, p. 55.
27. Flugel, J. C., "Men and their Motives", *Journal of the British Sexological Society*, 1934.
28. Riviere, J., in Klein, M., *et al.*, ed., *Developments in Psychoanalysis*, London, 1952.
29. Mowat, R. R., "Morbid jealousy and murder", in Glover, Mannheim and Miller, ed., *Delinquency and Deviant Social Behaviour*, International Library of Criminology, No. 11, London, 1966.
30. Freud, S., *Introductory Lectures on Psychoanalysis*, London, 1922.
31. Hadfield, J. A., *Psychology and Mental Health*, London, 1950, p. 385.
32. *Ibid.*, p. 380 f.
33. *Ibid.*, p. 372 f.
34. Healy, W., and Bronner, A., *New Light on Delinquency and its Treatment*, New Haven, 1936, p. 49.
35. East, *op. cit.*, p. 231.
36. Parker, T., and Allerton, R., *The Courage of his Convictions*, London, 1962.
37. Leopold, F. N., Jr., *Life Plus Ninety-nine Years*, London, 1958.
38. Fordham, M., *New Developments in Psychoanalysis*, London, 1957, p. 72.
39. Lorenz, K., *King Solomon's Ring*, London, 1952 and *On Aggression*, London, 1966, passim.
40. Jung, C. G., *Collected Works*, Vol. 8, London, 1960, p. 201.
41. Friedlander, *op. cit.*, p. 40.
42. Klein, M., *et al.*, *Developments in Psychoanalysis*, London, 1952, p. 210 ff.
43. Jung, C. G., *op. cit.*, p. 42.
44. Klein, *op. cit.*, p. 301. According to her Freud also recognized a "synthetic function".
45. Winnicott, D. W., *Collected Works*, London 1964, p. 4.
46. Fordham, M., *op. cit.*
47. Jung, *op. cit.*, Vol. 8, p. 530
48. For a full discussion of the relation between the instincts and archetypes see Jung's "Instinct and the unconscious", *Ibid.*, p. 210.
49. Fordham, *op. cit.*, p. 120.
50. For a clear exposition of the mechanisms of these early infantile experiences see Klein, M., *Envy and Gratitude*, London, 1957, and other writings. See also the articles by Joan Riviere and Melanie Klein in *Developments in Psychoanalysis*, London, 1952.

51. Cf., Winnicott, *Collected Papers*, London, 1958, p. 270: "The healthy child has a personal source of sense of guilt and need not be taught to feel guilty or concerned."

52. Mead, M., *Sex and Temperament in Primitive Societies*, London, 1935, p. 280.

53. John Bowlby, in his studies of delinquency, attributes some disastrous results to separation of parents before the child is five. See his "Research into the Origins of Delinquent Behaviour", *British Medical Journal*, 1950, p. 570 and "Maternal Care and Mental Health", *Bulletin of the World Health Organisation*, Vol. 3, No. 3, p. 355.

54. McCord, *op. cit.*

55. For further study on this question see Flugel, J. C., *Man, Morals and Society*, London, 1962. This is an exhaustive and eminently readable study of all aspects of the super-ego.

56. Burt, *op. cit.*, p. 188.

57. Glatt considers that "more important than alcoholism and the crimes committed by the alcoholic himself is the relationship between a parent's alcoholism and his children's insecurity. ... A parent's alcoholism cannot fail to have a far-reaching influence on his children's personality development". Glatt, M. M., "Alcoholism and Crime and Juvenile Delinquency", *British Journal of Crime and Delinquency*, 1958/9, p. 56.

58. Gibbens, T. C. N., *Psychiatric Study of Borstal Lads*, Maudsley Monograph Series, No. 11, London, 1963.

59. Flugel, *op. cit.* Here Flugel describes the many ways in which the super-ego is evaded or overcome in order to permit antisocial acts without consequent guilt feelings.

60. Gillespie, R. D., "Psychoneurosis and Criminal Behaviour", in Radzinowicz and Turner, *Mental Abnormality and Crime*, London, 1944.

61. Pearce. *op. cit.*

62. *Ibid.*, p. 197.

63. Jones, H., *Crime in a Changing Society*, London, 1965, p. 74.

64. East, *op. cit.*, p. 231–2

65. Friedlander, *op. cit.*, p. 27.

66. Burt, *op. cit.*, p. 14.

67. Brancale, R., *Law and Contemporary Problems*, Durham, 1958, p. 445.

68. Warren, W., "Conduct Disorders in Children", *British Journal of Delinquency*, London, 1950–1.

69. Roper, *op. cit.*, p. 27.

70. Gillespie, *op. cit.*, p. 82.

71. Burt, *op. cit.*, p. 581.

72. Jung, C. G., *op. cit.*, Vol. 16, p. 21.

73. Rees, J. R., ed., *Modern Practice in Psychological Medicine*, London, 1949, p. 381.

74. Published (Zürich, 1965) as "A Collection of Essays by Various

Hands, presented to Professor Meier, President of the Jung Institute in Zürich".

75. Fairbairn, W. R. D., *Psychoanalytic Studies of the Personality*, London, 1952, p. 13.
76. Friedlander, *op. cit.*, p. 192.
77. Reprinted *from Psychoanalytical Techniques*, New York, 1967.
78. Jung, C. G., *op. cit.*, Vol. 16.
79. *Ibid.*, p. 164.
80. The original article appeared in *Mental Hygiene*, Vol. 50, No. 3, July 1966.
81. Jung, *op. cit.*, Vol. 17, p. 44.
82. *Ibid.*, Vol. 11, p. 259.
83. Fordham, *op. cit.*, pp. 128, 118.
84. Jung, *op. cit.*, Vol. 12, p. 41.
85. Neumann, E., *The Origins and History of Consciousness*, London, 1954, pp. 270 and 321.
86. *Ibid.*, pp. 6–12.
87. Winnicott, D., *The Child, the Family and the Outside World*, Harmondsworth, 1964.
88. Neumann, *op. cit.* 32.
89. Winnicott, *op. cit.* 87. No better description of the happy mother/infant relationship can be found than in this collection of Winnicott's broadcast talks.
90. Jung, *op. cit.*, Vol. 12, p. 5.
91. *Ibid.*, p. 6.
92. *Ibid.*, Vol. 7, p. 236.
93. Neumann, *op. cit.*, p. xxiv.
94. Jung, *op. cit.*, Vol. 7, p. 133.
95. Harding, M. E., *Psychic Energy: its source and its transformation*, New York, 1963².

GLOSSARY

Some terms used by psychologists vary slightly according to their school of thought: some, again, are incorrectly used in popular speech. This glossary consists of technical terms which might be misinterpreted for these reasons. Where variations in meaning are given, it is Jung's use of the term which applies throughout this book.

Definitions are taken from the following works:

Jung, C. G., Glossary to *Memories, Dreams and Reflections* (MDR)
Jung, C. G., *Collected Works* (CW)
Shorter Oxford English Dictionary, 3rd Edn. (SOED)
Drever, J., *Dictionary of Psychology* (DOP)
Fordham, F., *Introduction to Jung's Psychology* (IJP)

In cases where definitions from these works were too long or technical, or too limited, I am indebted to Dr. Fay Pye, Dr. Smart's friend and also Jungian practitioner, for supplementing, or in a few cases, supplying a definition. The initials FP will follow in these cases.

Active imagination. A sequence of phantasies produced by deliberate concentration (i.e. in writing, painting etc.) (CW)

Anima and Animus. Personification of the feminine nature of a man's unconscious and the masculine nature of a woman's. Thus psychological bisexuality is a reflection of the biological fact that it is the larger number of male (or female) genes which is the decisive factor in the determination of sex. The smaller number of contrasexual genes seems to produce a corresponding contrasexual character which usually remains unconscious. Anima and Animus manifest themselves most typically in personified form as figures in dreams and fantasies ("dream-girl", "dream-lover"), or in the irrationalities of a man's *feeling* and a woman's *thinking*. As regulators of behaviour they are two of the most influential archetypes. (MDR)

Archetype. The concept of the archetype is derived from the repeated observation that, for instance, the myths and fairy tales of world literature contain definite motifs which crop up everywhere. We meet these same motifs in the fantasies, dreams, deliria, and delusions of individuals living today. ... The more vivid they are, the more they will be coloured by particularly strong feeling-tones. ... They have their origin in the archetype which, in itself, is an irrepresentable, unconscious, pre-existent form that seems to be part of the inherited structure of the psyche and can therefore manifest itself spontaneously anywhere, at any time. (MDR)

Differentiation. The process, or the result of the process, by which, in the course of development, a part, organ, etc., is modified into a special form or for a special function; specialization; also the gradual production of differences between the descendants of the same ancestral types. This term, describing a similar process of development and maturation is applied also to psychological functions such as thinking and feeling. (SOED/FP)

Fugue. A period of loss of memory, when the individual disappears from his usual haunts. (DOP)

Hieros gamos. Sacred or spiritual marriage, union of archetypal figures in the rebirth mysteries of antiquity and also in chemistry. Typical examples are the representation of Christ and the Church as bridegroom and bride (*sponsus et sponsa*) and the alchemical conjunction of sun and moon. (MDR)

Libido. Originally used by Freudian psychologists in the sense of sexual desire but by Jung and many later psychologists in a much wider sense. According to Jung, "We would be better advised ... to understand it as an energy value which is able to communicate itself to any field of activity whatsoever, be it power, hunger, hatred, sexuality or religion, without ever being itself a specific interest." (SOED/FP/CW Vol. 5)

Oedipus complex. The term is used in analysis to designate the unconscious, sexually-toned attachment of the son to the mother with resulting feelings of guilt and jealousy towards the father (corresponding to the Greek myth of Oedipus who killed his father and married his mother). This complex was thought by Freud to be universal. Jung doubted its universality as a strongly motivating factor. (DOP/FP)

Persona. In ancient Greek drama, the persona was the mask worn by an actor to represent the part he played: hence in Jung's psychology, the outward appearance that an individual presents to society. (CW/FP)

Personality disorder. A general psychiatric term used to describe the condition of individuals who consistently exhibit symptoms of maladaptation but who are not severely psychotic or suffering from organic disease. (FP)

Projection. A psychological mechanism in which subjective contents are believed to be objectively present as attributes of another person. For instance, unconscious aggression, when it is projected, is experienced as the hostility of the other person. Similarly, the unconscious image of the ideal woman in the mind of a man may be attributed to an actual woman, whether it is appropriate or not. (FP)

Psyche. "In speaking of mind and mental activity, Jung has chosen the term, psyche and psychic, rather than mind and mental, since the latter are associated primarily with consciousness, whereas psyche and psychic are used to cover both consciousness and the unconscious." (IJP)

"I am of the opinion that the psyche is the most tremendous fact of human life. Indeed, it is the mother of all human facts: of civilization and of its destroyer, war." (CW Vol.9)

Psychopath. An individual is said to be a psychopath when his personality is emotionally unstable and morally irresponsible but when his condition cannot be classified in other specific psychiatric terms. With such people the condition appears to be constitutional. (DOP/FP)

Psychosis. Used to designate certain kinds of mental disorder such as schizophrenia and manic depression, the symptoms of which were recognized by psychiatry as syndromes or disease entities. A psychosis differs from a neurosis in that the latter is known to be acquired, is accompanied by insight, and is accessible to psychotherapeutic treatment. Certain mental conditions in which the patient lacks insight are related to the psychoses. (SOED/FP)

Puer Aeternus. Latin term meaning the Eternal Boy. Jung used this term to describe a psychological condition in a male. "He is a child, a boy, the 'puer aeternus' of the immemorial prototype, heralding by his youth the resurrection and rebirth of all that was lost." (Jung: *Psychological Types*/ FP)

Shadow. The inferior part of the personality; sum of all personal and collective psychic elements which, because of their incompatibility with the chosen conscious attitude, are denied expression in conscious life and therefore coalesce into a relatively autonomous "splinter personality" with contrary tendencies in the unconscious. The shadow behaves compensatorily to consciousness; hence its effects can be positive as well as negative. (MDR)

Transference. A techical term used by analysts to describe the emotional attitudes of the patient to the analyst. Transference is an aspect of projection. A patient in a state of emotional dependence will project upon the analyst the positive or negative image of the mother. (FP)

BIBLIOGRAPHY

THIS LIST consists of the books and articles from which passages were transcribed by Dr. Smart in her notebooks of quotations and references—excluding those to which she referred in the text, of which particulars are given in the references. It does not comprehend all the books she consulted or was familiar with (even the books quoted in the text do not always appear in the notebooks). This list therefore should not be taken as exhaustive, though it is useful for further reading. The inclusion of a book does not, in every case, imply her agreement with the writer's theories: many of these books were consulted for evidence of observed facts.

Bouger, W. A., *Race and Crime*, Dr. Hordyk, M. M., New York, 1943.

Cohen, A. K., *Delinquent Boys*, London, 1956.

Curran, "Psychiatric Approach to Offenders" *Roots of Crime*, Ed. East, N., London, 1954.

Docker-Drysdale, P., "Residential Treatment of 'Frozen Children'", (*Brit. Journal of Delinquency*, Vol. 9, 2, 106).

Ferguson, Sir L., *English Prisons and Borstal Systems*, London, 1952.

Guirdham, A., *The Nature of Healing*, London, 1964.

Howard, D. L., *The English Prisons*, London, 1960.

Jackson, L., *Aggression and Interpretation*, London, 1954.

Joseph, B., "Some Characteristics of the Psychopathic Personality", *Journal of Psychoanalysis*, XLI, 1960.

Klare, H. J., *Anatomy of Prison*, London, 1960.

Klein, M., Ed., *Developments in Psychoanalysis*, London, 1952.

Lange, J., *Crime as Destiny*, London, 1931.

Mackwood, J., "Psychotherapy during Penal Detention", in *Roots of Crime (op. cit.)*.

Meade, J. E. and Parkes, A. S., Ed. *Genetic and Environmental Factors in Human Activity*, London, 1965.

Morris, P., *Prisoners and their Families*, London, 1965.

Radzinowicz, L., and Turner, J. W. C., Eds., *Mental Abnormality and Crime*, Cambridge, 1944.

Rich, J., "Types of Stealing", *Lancet*, pp. 496–8. Vol. I, 1957.

Reports of Prison Commissioners (quoted in notebooks from 1932–46).

Schmideberg, M., "Is the Criminal Amoral?" *Brit. Journ. of Delinquency*, Vol. IV. 4. 272.

Schmideberg, M., "Treating the Unwilling Patient", *Brit. Journ. of Delinquency*, Vol. IX. 2. 117.

Scott, P., "Clinical Contributions", in *Roots of Crime (op. cit.)*.

Suttie, I., *Origins of Love and Hate*, London, 1935.

Thompson, G., "Abnormal Psychology in Relation to Emotional Development", in *Modern Practice in Psychological Medicine*, Ed. Rees, J. R., London, 1949.

Zulliger, H., "Unconscious Motives for Theft", *Brit. Jour. of Delinquency*, I.3. 198–304.

INDEX